The Post Office Shop

K.T. DADY

The Post Office Shop
K.T. Dady

Life changes when you change.

4

1

Rory

Dreamcatcher Farm smelled like manure, not that Rory was expecting any other smell to come from a farm, but still. The strong odour burning his nostrils was causing his gag reflex to wake up, and there was no way he was about to throw up in front of the owner who had just kindly given him a job as a farmhand.

He glanced over at another field to see a small caravan park that belonged to the farm and wondered how it attracted any holidaymakers during the summer, with the foul smell lingering in the air. Maybe they weren't fussy. Maybe they liked farming, picking fruit, and growing veg. Maybe they were escaping reality, like him.

Mr Sheridan was pointing towards a large greenhouse, explaining something about seedlings, but Rory's mind had drifted away from the old man with the grey beard.

It's beautiful here. Look at all this land. I can't believe I'm actually standing in such a place. I feel like I'm in a dream. I know it's only the Isle of Wight, but still. Never thought about coming here before. I guess Nik knows what he's talking about. If he says this place will be good for me, then who am I to argue with the man. He knows his business. I'm just going to keep my head down and get the job done. New start. New life.

The open space around him was filling his heart with a humbleness and a level of gratitude he had never felt before. It had been fifteen years since he had the luxury of freedom. His mind kept jolting between serenity and surreal.

After the robbery that went oh so wrong back when he was thirty-four, Rory had seen little of the world. A twenty-year sentence reduced to fifteen made sure of that. Not much changed for him at first. Prison didn't scare him nor did it help dampen his cocky ways. It was all just one big game where nobody cared who the loser was, and Rory had felt like a loser all his life. He was called it often enough by the woman his dad married. God, he hated her. He also felt sorry for her at times. Something must have happened in her life to make her turn out so cruel. He thought it was a shame at times. He'd look at her and just know that she would never change. As a grown man, he often wondered if he would ever change.

Something about him did change one day. It was during his fourth year inside prison. A counsellor called Nik started mentoring him. They would talk so much, and everything Nik said made sense. He said there were two Rory's. The authentic one, and the one who was created by trauma.

Born in London to a young Irish couple filled with hopes and dreams of a new life in England, Rory had a good start. Nobody expected his mother's heart to suddenly stop beating one night whilst in her early twenties, especially as she seemed to be the picture of health. He was only two when his father took him to Ireland after his mum died, and life wasn't too bad in Cork at first. Within a year, he gained a new mother and four step-siblings, all of who seemed to hate his guts for some reason. What started out as a second chance at a family ended up with him living like some sort of Cinderella.

'So you get a clip round the ear from time to time, son. Don't we all,' his father would say whenever Rory tried to tell him of his step-mother's cruelty.

Rory took the beatings from the woman and lived a quiet existence, keeping mainly to himself. His life changing once again when his father was killed during a fight outside a pub one night. So, off he was sent back to London to live with his aunt. At the age of fourteen, he was expected to act like a man and look after himself.

'Because no one else sure as hell is going to hold your hand, Rory Murphy,' were his aunt's flat words on the subject.

Rory couldn't remember a time when anyone held his hand anyway, so it was no skin off his nose.

'God helps those who help themselves,' his aunt would say.

Rory took that particular advice to heart and helped himself plenty, mostly to things that weren't his. It was completely acceptable behaviour, according to his aunt's boyfriend. It helped put food on the table, so a blind eye was turned quite often, if not all the time.

Aunt Jean's other half, Tim, was the Irish equivalent of Bill Sikes, and Rory was quickly trained in the art of criminal shenanigans, whether he liked it or not.

Once Nik introduced the idea that Rory had been forced into a costume that never really fitted, Rory felt the layers fall away. Things suddenly started to make sense about his life. There was a reason he was so torn within. Why he fought with himself, hated himself, and why he always felt he was constantly searching for something that seemed just out of reach. Coldness and crime were installed, but not by him. He was a victim of his circumstances. If left alone, he probably would have grown into the man his mother would have raised him to be. That man was always in there, but the outside forces at work overruled him at every turn, creating someone else. Rory felt as though he could finally breathe again once Nik had explained the psychology.

From then on, Rory slowly rebuilt his personality, bit by bit, piece by piece, feeling his authentic-self return. At least, he was more comfortable with his life. Maybe it was Nik's help, or maybe being locked away with a schedule, routine, and some weird sort of stability changed him over time.

Rory took to psychology, studying the mind as much as he could and ended up helping the younger offenders come to terms with the science behind the chaos in their life.

The name of the organisation that helped ex-criminals was called Shine, and it was where Nik worked, and where Rory was introduced to Joseph Sheridan, who was seventy-seven, tall, grey, and fitter than a butcher's dog.

'You're forty-nine, Rory. You're going to be expected to work now you're out,' Nik had told him on release day. 'Dreamcatcher Farm has always worked closely with us. Not many hire those with a record like yours, so this is a good opportunity for you to have something positive for your CV.'

Never in a million years had Rory ever thought about being a farmer, but beggars can't be choosers. He knew that saying. The farm work had many bonuses. There was free accommodation, understanding folk, and so much space to roam freely.

Joseph gestured towards a row of three small houses joined together. 'Used to be stables, but we had them converted into homes. Nothing fancy, I'm afraid, just three small cottages, but they do the job.'

Rory stepped inside the grey building to see a snug living room with an open fireplace, a kitchenette to one side, and a narrow stairway heading up to the next level.

So, this is my new home. For now. Looks okay, but after fifteen years in a cell, he could have offered me the barn and

I would be grateful. Can't say I've ever had my own home before. I like it. Feels nice in here.

'There's heating and hot water,' said Joseph. 'A log fire. Wood's outside. Upstairs only has a small bathroom and one bedroom. It has a double bed.' He grinned widely through his wiry beard. 'We get big men like yourself from time to time. It made sense for us to put in the bigger beds.'

'You're very thoughtful, sir.'

'Call me Joseph, just don't shorten it to Joe.'

'I'll remember that.'

Joseph walked over to the kitchenette. 'We've supplied you with the basics, but you can pick up whatever extras you need once you get paid. Wages aren't much, but this place is free, and we're only really here to help give you a leg-up, Rory lad.'

'I understand. Nik explained everything.'

'Did he explain about the early starts and long days?'

Rory breathed out a laugh through his nose. 'He did, aye.'

'As it's autumn, we don't have any guests staying in the vans. We only get bookings for the summer. People like a bit of fruit picking and feeding the hens but shy away when the weather turns. Hotels are preferred around here then. You'll still help to maintain the area around the vans. Not that there's much going on. We have six caravans and a small play area for the little ones.'

'This is a new world for me, you know that, right?'

'It's a new world for most who come here, Rory lad, but you'll learn soon enough. A bit of maintenance work, collecting eggs, a lot of what you might call gardening, and keeping this place clean will get you started.' Joseph gestured to the small fridge next to the sink. 'We don't encourage alcohol here, son, but I won't begrudge you the odd cider up at the house on a Friday night.'

Rory was gasping for a cuppa and little else. 'I haven't had a drink in fifteen years, Joseph. I think I'll be leaving it alone for good now.'

'I'll leave you to it then. All that's left to say is welcome to my home. Hope you treat it and my family with the respect we deserve, and I really hope it all works out for you, Rory lad.'

Rory shook Joseph's hand and followed him outside. 'Thank you, sir. I really appreciate all that you're doing here for me and others like myself. You're a good man, and I won't let you down. I don't know what would make someone get into doing something like this for people like me, but I'm glad it's what you and your family do.'

'Ah, well, my son-in-law used to work for Shine, you see. He wasn't actually married to my daughter, but they were together for years, so we just called him that. He was the one who got us involved.'

'Does he not work there anymore?'

'He died, Rory lad. Stabbed during an altercation with a young offender at Shine about four years ago now. Nearly shut the place down, but we fought hard to keep it up and running. It would have been what Lucas wanted.'

'Sorry to hear that, sir.'

Joseph smiled softly and nodded. He glanced down a wide pathway made by tyre tracks and hard, clumpy mud. 'There's a small shop down there, which we own. It's called The Post Office Shop. Does what it says on the sign. Part post office, part shop. Sells the basic essentials, and if you get in there early enough, you can get your hands on some freshly baked bread. My daughter runs the place. She makes some loaves first thing. Pop in anytime you like. She'll help you find anything you need. We're a friendly bunch here in Pepper Bay, as you'll soon find out.'

'Thank you. I'll be sure to pop over there whenever I need anything.'

Joseph stalled for a moment. 'Erm... about my daughter. After Lucas, she didn't want any more ex-offenders working up here. So, we didn't have any for the first year, and you're the third one we've had since we started back. She's a friendly girl, and she won't tell anyone about your backstory, as we never do. You're just another farmhand come to help out. Nobody need know your business, Rory lad. It's just, she might not be as personable as the rest of the family, but she won't be rude to you or anything like that. I just wanted you to have an understanding towards her. Be gentle.'

In other words, leave my daughter alone.

'I understand. You have my word, I'll be kind, Joseph. She won't get bother from me. I'll keep out of her way.'

'That won't be that easy. I want you up at the shop first thing, sanding the window ledges. They need a good lick of paint, and that can be your first job around here.'

2

'What is that noise?' The clattering sound coming from outside The Post Office Shop was starting to annoy Tilly to the max. She put the rest of the tins of beans on the shelf and turned to the small square window by the counter. Wiping her hands down her blue dungarees, she made her way over to the old wooden shop door and stepped out at the same time a big burly man walked in.

'Oof!' She bounced back slightly and large hands grabbed her waist.

'Sorry, are you all right?'

Tilly's big chocolate eyes rolled up the solid chest facing her to meet with grey-blue eyes, greying dark hair and a short neatly-trimmed beard, and a possible Paul Newman stunt double. 'Erm…'

He dropped his hands. 'I was just coming inside to let you know I'm about to start work on the window ledges.'

His soft Irish accent disorientated her for a moment, that and the fact that no one had told her about any maintenance work taking place.

'Are you all right?' he asked again. 'Did I hurt you at all?'

She slowly shook her head whilst staring at the breadth of his shoulders. Well aware she was starting to look like a prize idiot.

Speak, woman. What's wrong with you?

'You just made me jump, that's all,' she managed to blurt out, trying to avoid those grey-blues that appeared more grey than blue on closer inspection. Not that she was staring again.

'Sorry about that. I'm guessing you're Matilda Sheridan, Joseph's daughter, who runs this place.'

'Tilly. And you are?'

'Rory Murphy. New farmhand.'

'Oh.'

He lowered his eyes and started twiddling with the hem on his tee-shirt, displaying nerves usually reserved for kids waiting outside the head teacher's office for a stern talking-to and possible suspension. 'So, I'll just get to it then. Best to get on while the weather is still warm and dry.'

'Yes, it's a nice September. Although, September has only just started, so we don't really know how it's going to go.'

'Aye.'

Neither of them moved away, and Tilly wasn't quite sure why her legs weren't working or why she had just rambled on about September.

'I'll make you a cup of tea, if you like,' she offered, not knowing what else to say.

Could I be any more British? Weather. Tea. Flipping heck, let the man get back to work. And why am I even involving myself? Do what you normally do, Tilly, walk away from the farmhand.

'That would be grand.' He smiled weakly.

'Have you eaten? It's early. I wasn't sure if you've had any breakfast yet.'

Oh God, now I sound like my mum. Stop talking. Walk away. Make the blimming tea. You've offered now.

'Erm, that's all right. I've had breakfast. Thanks all the same. Kind of you to offer, Miss Sheridan.'

'Tilly.'

He gave a nod. 'Tilly.'

She slumped her shoulders and exhaled as soon as he went back outside, not realising she had breath she was holding on to. Sauntering down the toiletry aisle, she stopped to faff about with the loo roll whilst casually glancing at the ladder leaning against the window by the door. There were definite muscles going on beneath the pair of jeans that were visible, that much was obvious.

Flipping heck. How gorgeous is he? We've never had an ex-crim here that looked like that before. Not that it matters what he looks like. He's still from Shine. He's still... Oh, I can't think that way. He's done his time. He's moving on with his life. That's what Lucas was most proud of. Helping people move forward. I'll give him a chance. After all, he seemed friendly enough. He must have worked-out inside. He's not overly big, but he's definitely solid under those clothes. I like his legs.

She turned sharply when his boots moved down a couple of rungs. There was no way she wanted to get caught ogling his legs. Sparkles were the first thing that she saw after her head connected with a metal shelf, then came the noise of falling products. Tilly sat up at the same time that Rory appeared.

'Ah, Jesus, are you all right, Tilly?'

Slightly dazed, she glanced around at the incontinence pads and dandruff shampoo that she could see surrounding her.

Rory was on his knees, picking up bottles of hair removal foam from her lap. 'Let me help you.'

'I... erm.'

His hand was suddenly resting on the side of her dark, shoulder-length, wavy hair. 'Did you hit your head?'

She raised her hand to his, mindlessly linking her fingers with his own. 'I think I did.'

His soft eyes were gazing at her brow. 'Aye, you did. There's a small bump coming up already. Do you have a freezer in here? We need to put something cold on it straight away.'

She pointed behind her, even though the small chest freezer was in the opposite direction. Rory found it anyway, and before she could say another word, a small bag of petits pois was pressed against her head. 'I won't be able to sell them now.'

He smiled directly into her eyes. 'I'll buy them. You'll have to give me credit though. I don't get paid till the end of the week.'

They both laughed, and Tilly winced.

'How about I sit you down in a chair and I go make you some tea?' he offered.

She guided him to the back of the shop where a wide kitchen led to a back garden filled with herbs, a winding pathway, and a small greenhouse.

Rory arched his brow. 'This place looks a lot smaller from the outside.'

'That's because you can't see around the back from out front, thanks to the trees around the side.'

'It really is a quaint little place, isn't it? I love the square windows. It's like a little country cottage, not a shop at all. You could live here.'

'I do. Upstairs.'

He filled the bright yellow kettle and switched it on. 'I guess I would live here too, given the choice.'

She removed the frozen peas from her head, as water had started to drip down her bare arm, entering her three-quarter length pink tee-shirt sleeve. 'How do you like your little cottage? The three homes there used to be stables.'

'Aye. Your dad told me. It's a nice place. I'm grateful for the home and work.' He looked around for cups and pulled down one covered in ducks from a cupboard that she gestured towards. 'I'll sort you out, then get back to work. You don't need me hanging around.'

'It's okay. You're not in the way.'

'I know, but your dad told me...'

'Oh.'

Silence loomed for a moment that was neither awkward nor comfortable.

Rory handed her a piece of kitchen roll and examined her head again as though he were some sort of A&E doctor. 'I think you'll live.'

A woody scent wafted her way as he closed in on her now flushed face.

Mmm, he smells nice. Oh, no, bloody hell! Not now. Oh my G...

Her body started to heat faster than the water in the kettle. She blew out, what felt like, hot air, and rapidly fanned her cheeks.

Rory stepped back, seemingly assessing the situation. 'Are you all right, Tilly?'

'No,' she managed, fanning faster. She tugged the straps of her dungarees down and lifted her top, revealing her food baby and the yellow lace at the bottom of her M&S bra. One hand found the frozen peas on the side and quickly squashed them into her stomach. 'Oh my God!'

Rory looked just as flustered. 'Are you burning up?'

'Something like that. Are your hands cold?'

He glanced down at his palms. 'Erm...'

There wasn't any more time for a conversation. She grabbed his hand and forced it on her neck. His fingers were resting beneath the neckline of her tee-shirt, touching her collarbone. 'Oh God, that's lovely.' Shoving his hand that bit further towards her bra, she gasped out in delight again. His cool touch was helping just as much as the peas. 'Oh my God, Rory, that's so nice. Don't move. Oh, maybe move a bit. Find another spot. Touch my back.' He didn't get a chance to respond because she moved his hand for him, shoving it up her back. 'Oh, yeah, that's perfect.' She moaned out his name again as she closed her eyes and tipped her head back as though starring in her own erotic movie.

Where's an ice bath when you need one? Note to self. Google more about hot flushes.

A gentle breeze drifted down her neck, causing her sweat beads to cool. She lowered her chin to see where it was coming from, only to see Rory blowing on her skin. A small smile was tugging at the corners of his mouth, which made her automatically smile back.

'How you doing over there?' he whispered.

Like I've just returned from a daytrip to the Earth's core. I didn't wear flip flops, and there certainly wasn't any air con. No one handed out 99s, and water was just a figment of someone's imagination.

She started to control her breathing and took a calming breath. 'It's starting to pass now. I'm so sorry about that.'

'No need to be sorry.'

Flashes of the morning after flittered through her mind. The time she actually did do the walk of shame from a lad's house back when she was in her late teens. Her head was still groggy and her hair looked like she'd been electrocuted. And did he call? Did he heck! Her friends thought it was funny and welcomed her to the club. That wasn't any club she wanted a yearly membership to. Nope. Her one-night stand was definitely a one-off.

'I grabbed your hand and stuck it down my top.'

His smile widened and a soft twinkle hit his eyes. 'Well, it's been a while, so I'm not going to complain.'

She laughed and removed the peas. 'Flipping heck, that was so hot.'

'Erm, would you like me to move my hand away now?'

Not really. I know it's inappropriate, but it's been a while for me too. Oh, Tilly, what are you doing?

'Okay. Thank you for your help, even though I forced you into it.'

'Ah, it was… interesting.'

A shiver ran the full length of her spine as her normal temperature returned in full, causing her to quickly pull down her top and sort out her dungarees.

'Does that happen often?' he asked, taking a step back and giving her some room.

'Every now and then. It's a bit unpredictable. I don't even get a heads-up. It can be a bloody nightmare.'

She could see the mixture of amusement and confusion in his eyes. It was to be expected, after the stunt she just pulled.

'So, what was it, exactly? I mean, I guessed a hot flush, but you're a bit young for that, so now I'm wondering…'

'It was definitely a hot flush. They started about two years back. I'm older than I look. I'm the big 5 0 now.'

'No way. I'm not buying that. You're fifty?'

Tilly nodded. She was used to people not believing her about her age.

'You look thirty-five, if that.'

'We have young genes in my family. Well, we do on my mum's side. The men in our family aren't as blessed, but don't tell my brother I said that.'

'Well, you look good, Tilly Sheridan, so you do.'

'Even when I was on fire?'

Another sparkle hit his gentle eyes. 'Oh, especially when you were on fire.'

Tilly felt her stomach flip. She straightened up in her high-back kitchen chair and controlled the smile attempting to creep across her face. 'I really am sorry about sticking your hand down my top. My dad will go nuts if he finds out. We'll get hit with a sexual harassment in the workplace lawsuit or something.'

Rory gave a slight shake of the head. 'I won't be complaining to the police that you put my hand on your breast.'

She drooped her shoulders and waved a hand his way. 'I didn't put your hand on my breast.'

He gave a half-shrug and grinned. 'Close enough.'

'I was just so hot.'

'And you can give me a call anytime you feel hot.'

She laughed as she stood, pushing him away and ignoring how his chest felt under her palm. 'I won't be making a habit of this.'

'Aw, that's a shame, Tilly. I kind of liked the way you moaned out my name.'

'Oh hush. You can get back to work. I'll make the tea and fetch you one out in a minute.'

He chuckled as he walked away. 'It was nice meeting you this morning, Miss Sheridan.'

Tilly felt her cheeks heat, and this time she couldn't blame the menopause.

3

Rory

A smile built on Rory's face as he neared his new home after a long day's work to see Tilly standing outside. A tray was in her hands with two dishes on top, one wrapped in a lemon tea towel.

'And what are you doing waiting on my doorstep?' He held his palms up and wiggled his fingers. 'Have you come for use of my cold hands? They're a bit warm at the moment, but for you, I'll happily stick them in the freezer.'

Tilly smiled down at the food she was carrying. A pinkness about her cheeks made her cheery face even more welcoming. 'I wanted to apologise properly for this morning, so I made you a lasagne, and there's a mixed salad here too. You don't have to eat it tonight if you don't fancy it, but if you do, it's ready now.'

'Have you had your dinner yet?'

'No. I thought I'd bring this to you first.'

'Looks like there's plenty there. Do you want to join me?'

She entered his cottage as soon as he opened the door, causing him to laugh under his breath.

'Come in,' he mumbled to himself.

She was already setting up the small table for dinner before he had even closed the door. He turned to her and smiled widely at her confidence at being in his domain.

'Lucky I'm not a vegetarian.'

She smiled over her shoulder. 'Hey, I brought salad.'

He quickly washed his hands at the sink, then approached the table, chuckling as she shoved him down onto a chair. 'Oh, I'm sitting here, am I?'

She stopped moving for a second. 'Where would you like to sit?'

'Here's fine.'

A plate was placed in front of him and his dinner served. There was something comforting about the way she was fussing around him, as though she had been doing it for years. He pulled his lips in, trying not to laugh at her casualness.

'Thanks for doing this. You didn't have to. I already told you this morning that I wasn't going to press charges. You don't need to butter me up.' He watched her sit opposite him, scooping salad onto her plate. Her dark eyes were smiling just as much as her mouth.

'Oh, sod off, you. I'm being friendly. You did me a good turn earlier, so now I'm returning the favour.'

'Is that right? Well, I'd prefer a cool hand on my chest and...'

'You're getting a hot meal in your belly, and that's your lot, Murphy.'

Rory tipped his head. 'Yes, miss.' He tucked in to his homecooked meal, feeling full-on grateful that anyone had bothered to cook for him at all. It had been a long time since he sat at a table with a woman and enjoyed a decent meal.

'Do you like it?' she asked, shoving a slice of cucumber in her mouth whilst smiling.

He nodded and swallowed his food. 'You're a good cook, Tilly Sheridan, but I think you already know that, judging by the stupid grin wiped across your face.'

Her laughter warmed him as much as the hot food.

Now what? What do I say to her? She makes me laugh. I like her. Aye, let's get to know her. Why not?

'So, why don't you tell me about yourself, Tilly. Stuff I don't already know.'

People-reading was one of his skills. He learned a long time ago how to read a room. It was in his best interest to home in on energy changes and the slightest shift in the atmosphere, especially when he was in prison. What was he picking up on now? She was either stalling or couldn't think of anything to say.

'What you see is what you get,' she finally said, shrugging and continuing to eat. 'Your life is probably way more interesting,' she added, mouth full.

He stared at his fork, trying to decide whether to eat the food on it or talk about his life. 'My past is messy.' He shoved the food in his mouth, stopping himself from adding to his statement.

'That's okay. We don't have to talk about it. What are your plans for tomorrow?'

Wow, I thought she would press the matter. Well, if she can brush over it, so can I.

'Finish off your windows, I guess.'

'There'll be more variety than that soon. We have Harvest Festival coming up. It takes place in the town next door, Sandly. Hope Park is turned into one giant market for a weekend, and we have a stall where we sell our apples and veg. We also give some to the local foodbank. It's a fun day, all in all, filled with lots of activities. You'll enjoy that day out.'

'Will you be on the stall too, or do you just stay in the shop every day?'

'My mum works in the shop whenever we have market days. I've always helped out with the stalls, just to break up the monotony. It's normally me and my brother, Bobby. Have you met him yet?'

'Tall, built, greying beard, looks like your dad. I met him today. Is it just you two?'

Swallowing her food, she shook her head. 'No. I have two other brothers, both older than us. One lives in London, the other in Cardiff. They don't like farm life. We hardly see them anymore, which is sad for my mum. She misses them, but they have their own families and are happy enough. My nephew, Jamie, lives with my parents. You'll see him around. He's just turned fifteen. He's my eldest brother's kid. He came here because he was getting into all sorts of trouble in Cardiff. He's doing a lot better now. Farming is definitely in his blood. I had a little sister too, Luna, but she died when she was twenty-one. Cancer. I was twenty-seven back then. It was a long time ago.'

Rory stopped eating and rested his hand upon hers for a moment. 'I'm sorry you lost your sister, Tilly. That's a shite thing to happen to a family.'

She continued to eat her dinner as soon as he released her hand, and he wasn't entirely sure if she was showing signs of awkwardness for once.

'Have you got family, Rory?'

He thought about that for a second. Could he really call his poor excuse for relatives his family? They weren't exactly there for him, especially after he was locked up. The letters stopped after two years, and the visits long before that. He had spent many years feeling abandoned and alone. It was one of the reasons he was so keen to be of help to the younger lads who went to prison feeling alone and lost. He knew that feeling well and didn't like to see it in others.

'Just me,' he decided.

'You never had children?' she asked casually, although there seemed to be an edge to her voice, but he put that down to her having no shame in talking with her mouth full.

'No. You?'

She shook her head. 'We kept saying next year, next year and then we got too old. Well, I did. I wouldn't want to be an old mum, so that's that.'

Rory happily finished off the rest of his dinner. 'You'd make a fine wife, Tilly Sheridan. You know how to feed a man.'

'I'm not sure if that's sexist.'

He choked on the last morsel. 'Ah, you're killing me, miss. I'll tell you what I'll do. Tomorrow night, I'll do the cooking. Even out the score. Don't expect much. I'm a basic cook.'

A low grumbling came from her before she raised her head to look over at him. 'Oh, okay, maybe just this once.'

'I'm not that bad.'

She smiled warmly, and he liked the way her eyes came alive with affection. 'I don't mean it like that. It's just, I know how hard farm work is. My mum would tell me off for allowing you to cook for me after a day's work.'

'You work too.'

'Yes, but I was raised in a sexist environment.' She laughed. 'We Sheridan women look after our men.'

'But I'm not your man, Tilly, so I'm thinking it won't count.'

Ah, with that look she gave me, anyone would think I'd just punched her in the gut.

'But if those are the rules around here, who am I to argue,' he quickly added, hoping to see her smile reappear.

Tilly got up to get them some water from the fridge. She filled his glass, then her own and sat back down. 'I don't mean to come over all *wife* on you, Rory. It's just my way. It's how I was raised. I know you're independent, I…'

'Hey, it's okay. I've never had anyone fuss over me before. It's a bit of a novelty, if I'm to be honest about that. I'm having a nice night. Best meal I've ever had. Grand company too. Thank you for just… Well, thank you. I appreciate your sexist kindness.'

An eruption of giggles filled the small house as Tilly snorted the glass of water she had pressed to her lips.

Ah, Rory Murphy, you've got feelings for this girl already, haven't you? Jesus, just look away. Don't stare at her mouth.

Tilly stopped laughing and wiped her lips with the back of her hand. 'Oh, I didn't bring anything for afters.'

He gestured to a kitchen cupboard. 'I have a packet of choccy biscuits back there. Will that do?'

'I think I can manage one.'

'Maybe two?'

'Maybe.'

'I have an idea, Tilly. How about instead of dinner tomorrow night, we share lunch together instead. I've seen the shop's sign. You close for half an hour at noon. We can meet up then. The weather's going to be fine again, so I'm thinking a picnic somewhere around here. I've always wanted to go on a picnic, and I make a mean sandwich, so at least you'll be safe with that.'

Her brow was raised as high as it could go. 'You've never been on a picnic? Ever?'

'I once stole a picnic hamper. Does that count?'

'Only if you're Yogi Bear.'

He burst out laughing. 'I'm definitely not as smart as the average bear.'

'You're almost as big as one. Did you workout inside?'

He glanced at his forearm and noticed her eyes follow. 'I've always been tall and broad, but, aye, I did keep in shape in prison. Only because it's good for the mind.'

'It's made your body look good too.'

Ah, what am I going to do with this woman?

The grin spreading across his face was making him laugh more than her. 'Oh, well, thanks. It wasn't planned. It just happened along the way.'

'Sounds like life.'

'Aye. It does.'

Tilly cleared the table and started to wash up, but there was no way he was going to allow that. He went over to her and took her hands in his, removing them from the sink and turning off the tap.

'Do you ever stop, woman?'

She was looking down at their linked fingers, so he slipped his hands away, replacing them with a tea towel. She dried her hands and leaned against the sink, staring at him.

He knew a question was coming. It was written all over her face. 'What are you about to ask?'

'I was wondering what it's like in prison.'

Where to start with that? No doubt, like everyone else, she's watched Porridge or Shawshank, and wonders which is closer to the truth.

The fire could do with lighting, so he figured it was a good distraction from the question for all of five minutes. He made his way into the lounge and sat down, staring into the grate whilst deciding to choose his words carefully.

'I found it a weird place.' He turned sharply, jumping slightly, as she was suddenly by his side. 'Do you ask all us ex-crims that question?'

'No. Not asked anyone before.' She took the lighter from his hand and aimed it at some firelighter blocks that he hadn't noticed. 'You don't like talking about it, do you?'

He focused on her knee pressed against his whilst she sat there, cross-legged, staring into the building flames. 'It's not the best conversation.'

'This must feel weird for you too.'

The corners of his mouth twitched with amusement. 'What, sitting in front of an open fire with a woman I barely know who likes the look of my body, feeds me dinner, and has already moaned out my name? Yeah, it's a little strange.'

Tilly snorted out a laugh as she nudged his arm. 'Oi! I did not moan out your name.'

'You totally did.'

They shared a smile, then she stood. 'I'm going to leave you to it. I have to be up early.'

'Ah, yes, you make bread in the morning.'

'Not for much longer. The kneading hurts my hands now.'

'I could come over and help with that, if you like?'

There was sarcasm in her arched eyebrows. 'Really?'

'Aye. I can knead, thank you very much. It's not exactly rocket science, I'll have you know.'

'You'll have to come over at four, and you start work with my dad at six.'

'That's two hours you'll have me for to do with what you will.'

Oh, that's a naughty grin you have about you there, Miss Sheridan. Ah, I think the lack of women in my life for the last fifteen years is starting to go to my head.

She headed for the door, and he was quick to open it for her. The porch light illuminated her wavy hair and created a sparkle in her big chocolate eyes.

27

'You should get some sleep.' She poked his chest, causing some sort of weird fizz to hit his stomach. 'I always have an early night, and it will do you good too. I'm pretty much going straight to bed when I get in.'

'Do you want some company?'

Her laugh was infectious. He joined in as he closed the door behind them.

'Does that line actually work?'

He gave a half-shrug. 'Can't remember, but your mind's in the wrong place. I was talking about walking you home.'

She fell into step beside him. 'Sure you were.'

'Hey, I'm a gentleman, I'll have you know.'

'Don't tell me, all Irishmen are.'

'Aye, but I'll let you into a little secret. I'm actually English. I was born in London, then raised in Ireland.'

'So your parents were Londoners?'

'No, Irish through and through. They went there to start a new life. My dad had work there, you see.'

She nodded and playfully leant into his arm. 'I think we can safely say that you are way more Irish than you are English.'

'Aye, that's true.'

'You know, you don't have to walk me home. This is my land. I'm pretty safe.'

Rory stumbled in a ditch in the walkway.

Tilly giggled as she grabbed his arm to help steady him. 'You, on the other hand, might need some help.'

Before she had a chance to remove her hand from his arm, he held it in his. 'You're right. Best to hold my hand to be sure.'

They reached the shop, and Tilly led him around to the back door.

'I'm not inviting you in for coffee, you know.'

'I wasn't expecting you to, and just so you know, if you had, I would've said no, on account that I'm not that easy, I'll have you know, Miss Sheridan.'

'Oh, is that right?'

''Tis.'

Her cheek felt warm beneath his lips as he said his goodnight. 'Thank you for dinner, Tilly. I'll see you bright and early.' He waited until he heard her lock the door, then he turned away.

The walk back seemed even darker, for some strange reason, making him fully awake to his surroundings. The odd glance over his shoulder and the wary feeling in his gut reminded him that he was definitely an outsider.

Crickets were the only sound, a waft of manure the only smell, and darker than dark the only sight. Even before he was used to the noise of prison, he only knew police sirens and burglar alarms. Walking the streets of London late at night felt way more comfortable. Noisy traffic, the odd drunk, and occasional fight. It all felt more soothing than creepy open farmland.

His heart was pumping a lot faster than normal, and he wasn't paying too much attention to the path ahead. He stumbled into a tree, fell down another crack in the ground, and jumped when something squawked nearby, but he somehow managed to find his way home and was relieved to do so.

He closed the front door, took a breath, stared over at the dishes in the sink, and shook his head whilst breathing out a laugh. 'Oh, Rory Murphy, what is happening in your life now?'

4

Tilly

Straightening out the corners of the picnic blanket, Tilly smiled to herself with thoughts about her unusual half an hour lunch break. Normally, she'd sit out the back of the shop by herself and read a cosy mystery whilst eating whatever she fancied that day. True crime wasn't an interest until the hot Irish Londoner turned up. He oozed confidence and charm, in amongst a humbleness that shone through his grey-blue eyes. She decided she liked his eyes the first moment she saw them twinkle her way. There was a kindness behind them that seemed so far away from a life of crime. Her gut instinct was telling her that she was sitting with a good-natured man, but her mind reminded her of his past.

I wonder if it's worth asking him about his past now. I know I can get details from Dad. Nik has to let him know about what crime was committed. There's no way we'd open our doors to anyone. I don't want to go behind Rory's back though. I want him to be the one who tells me. Why am I so interested anyway? Why not? Why shouldn't I know? I have a right. Sod it. I'm asking.

'Will you tell me about your past, Rory?'

He shuffled on the blanket, removing food items from the wicker basket she had supplied. 'Which part?'

'I want to know what crime you committed.'

'Aye. Well, that's fair enough. You wouldn't want to be sitting here having a picnic with a mad axeman.'

30

Tilly snorted out a laugh. 'Good grief, what a thought.' She watched the smile fade from his face.

'Robbery,' he said quietly.

'How long did you do inside?'

'Fifteen stretch.'

'Wow, that's a long time.'

'Somebody died during the robbery.'

Without realising, she shifted her body slightly away from him. She picked up a plate and started to pick out some sandwiches from a plastic container.

Rory's head bobbed. 'Yeah, I can see that's made you feel uncomfortable, but just so you know, I didn't kill the man.'

The rest of the story needed to be heard in order for her to relax, otherwise she was ready to pack up and leave. Lucas was already at the front of her mind, but it was also because of him that she was willing to give Rory the moment to explain.

'Erm, the getaway driver ran over a fella passing by.' He looked down at his knee as it twitched, then he started to twiddle a pink napkin in his left hand. 'It was an accident, but we didn't stop. It was a chaotic moment and...'

Tilly glanced at him when his voice faded. There was nothing about him that she recognised. All of his cheeky charm and big smile had been replaced with sadness and remorse. It was crystal clear he had regrets.

Rory took a deep breath as he scratched at his short beard, then he started to pack the picnic away.

She quickly placed her hand over the basket. 'Whoa, what are you doing?'

'This was a bad idea. You don't need to be hanging around with someone like me. I'm heading back to work.'

'No, please, don't. Wait. Just wait a moment.' She moved her hand to rest it down upon his knee, and he stilled. 'I know

31

your past isn't nice, but it is your past. Obviously, you're not that man anymore, or you wouldn't be here.'

His eyes rolled up to meet hers. 'I served my time, Tilly. I changed the man I was. I can't relate to that person back then. He is so far from me, but an innocent man died because of our selfishness and that will haunt me to the day I die.'

'I'm not trying to excuse what happened, but you weren't the one who killed him.'

'It doesn't make any difference. I was still in the van. I didn't ask the driver to stop.'

'Would he have?'

'No. Not in a million years.'

'So, it was out of your hands.'

Rory smiled weakly at her. 'You're being kind, Tilly, but we both know I was a part of that robbery. It's a joint effort. That's the way it played out in court.'

'Did you all get the same sentence?'

He shook his head and avoided eye contact by looking around the field. 'The driver got the longest, and another fella got longer for carrying a weapon. The other two got the same as me.'

A moment of silence lingered between them. A cool breeze made its way through the warm air, causing Tilly to remove her brown cardigan from her waist and slip it on, covering the top half of her dark-red dungarees. She reached over and held his hand, feeling he needed it holding.

'I'm glad you're not that person anymore, Rory.'

She was pleased to see a familiar gleam hit his eye. That was the look she had got used to seeing already. Today was the first time she had met the sadness in him. She didn't like that look. He had been so cheery since their first encounter. She hoped to see that side of him again and nothing else.

'I'm glad too, Tilly.'

'I'm sorry I brought up your past when you don't live there anymore. I'm not into back-shaming or anything. I just wanted to know.'

He squeezed her hand gently. 'Hey, you have every right to know who you're breaking bread with.'

'I do know him. Well, I'm getting to know him, and I don't think he's that man you just told me about.'

'No. That man no longer exists. I can promise you that. I'd often talk about the past and back-shaming with the younger lads inside. I understand that everyone has a past, but if you've moved on, then that should be the focal point. Some of the lads would worry that they'd never be able to live, what we call, a normal life after prison. That's why I'm against back-shaming. It teaches nothing. Kids need to know that they can mess up and learn from their mistakes, rather than be held accountable for them forever. It's tricky when you've committed crimes. Not many want to let you move on from that life. I'm grateful to those who hand out second chances. God knows we all need them.'

The atmosphere feels off now. I had to ask though. It shouldn't really make me feel bad. He didn't kill anyone. That's a plus. He's right about back-shaming. People do that all the time. I'm not the same person I was five years ago, so I can't expect anyone else to be either. I'm glad he learned lessons and changed his attitude. What's the point of anything if we never learn and grow? Oh, what a tangled web we weave. I feel so blessed for my life now. He doesn't have the best backstory. I bet there's so much more to find out about his past. Now's not the time.

'Shall we eat your sandwiches now and talk about something else?'

'That would be grand. What should be our next riveting subject?'

She breathed out a laugh through her nose and bit into a ham sandwich. 'Hmm, your sandwich-making skills.'

He laughed, making everything feel normal again. 'Hey, I told you this morning that lunch would be good, and by the way, my fingers have been aching all day from kneading that dough this morning, so it took a lot of effort making those sandwiches, hope you know.'

She swallowed a mouthful. 'I appreciate it. Thanks.' She followed his eyes over the grass.

'Tell me about this area, Tilly.'

'It's called Wishing Point, and it's a big picnic spot during the summer.' She pointed uphill. 'If you walk straight to the top and turn that way, you get to the clifftop. So that's nice if you like a sea view, rather than Pepper River down here.'

'Does the name have anything to do with all these dandelion seed heads around us?'

'Aye.'

He laughed. 'Oh, that's funny. Mocking me already. Now I know we must be friends.'

She smiled and went back to eating.

'So, have you made any wishes lately?' he asked, picking one from the grass to his side.

'I haven't made a wish in years.'

He offered her the seed head. 'Here. Go on. Make a wish.'

Tilly took a swig of water from a bottle, then blew the tiny particles of the plant whilst he was still holding it. She smiled as they blew away into the light breeze.

I wish you peace, Rory Murphy.

'Well?' he asked. 'What did you wish for?'

'Come on, you know the rules.'

'Okay. Fair enough.'

'Your turn.'

He picked another one and blew. His eyes sparkled her way, and Tilly felt her heart warm at the way he was looking at her.

His grin widened. 'Admit it, you're dying to know what I wished for.'

'No, I'm not,' she lied.

He laughed and tucked into some food.

'How long will you be here for?' she asked.

'Not sure. How long does anyone stay here?'

'It varies. The longest we've had was seven months, and the shortest was six weeks. We know we're not a long-term solution for anyone. It is all about how farming works out for them, I guess. It's an acquired taste, as my mum would say. It's only really designed as a leg-up, so we don't have expectations, but if anyone did want to stay for a long time, they'd be welcome.'

Why did I say it like that? It sounded like I was inviting him to stick around. I'll admit, I want him to. Oh my goodness, I actually want him to.

Warmth in his gaze made the smile she was holding back appear.

'So, why is it called Dreamcatcher Farm? Any story behind that?'

Thoughts of how much her parents loved each other filled her heart. They had given her such a wonderful upbringing. She had so many happy memories to fall back on whenever needed.

'It used to be called Dream Land Farm, but my dad changed the name as a wedding gift to my mum. He also gave her half the farm. She has always made dreamcatchers, you see. She used to sell them at markets when she was younger, and now my nephew helps her sell them online. We've all got one hanging above our bed.'

'Aye, I've seen mine. Green, white, and yellow, it is.'

'Mine's white with a hint of beige.'

'That's a sweet thing that your dad did for your mum.'

Tilly knew she was made from pure love. It warmed her to remember. 'He loves her very much.'

Rory stared at her for a moment, then glanced around. 'So, what else is around here?'

She gestured her head down towards the river. 'Well, there's a tram that runs along there that goes between Pepper Bay and Sandly.'

Rory followed her hand movements as she continued. 'The dirt track out the front of my shop takes you to Pepper Lane, where you'll find loads of chocolate box cottages. And, down the bottom end are a few quaint shops, a family pub, and a small shingle beach.'

Rory glanced over his shoulder. 'Anything else?'

'The road between here and Pepper Lane is called Walk Walk Road, but don't ask me why. Everyone asks. Nobody knows. I think it started off as a nickname. Then, over in Sandly, you have a bit more life. It's the nearest big town to us, and it has a beautiful golden stretch of sand.' She pointed forward. 'Just up the road there are two small hotels. It used to be one, but it got split in two after the owners fell out many moons ago. Only one is up and running properly. You can always pop over there for a meal. They have a great chef, or if you fancy a coffee and slice of cake, then Edith's Tearoom in Pepper Lane is the place to go, or The Ugly Duckling pub does nice food.'

'Sounds like I might need to explore. Especially, if I am considering sticking around for a while.'

Tilly felt herself smile on the inside. She quickly dusted off the feeling. 'Oh, you've only been here five minutes. I'm sure you'll get bored soon enough.'

'Oh, I don't know. So far, it's been quite entertaining.'

5

Rory

A week had passed, and Rory was enjoying his time spent on Dreamcatcher Farm more and more every day. Being surrounded by nature was therapeutic, and seeing Tilly each day helped everything feel better. He had taken to guessing which colour dungarees she would be wearing the next day, as it seemed to be her preferred choice of clothing.

He entered the farmhouse kitchen, stomping over the stone floor with his dark wellies. He felt exhausted from washing down caravans, fixing wobbly fence posts, and trying to catch a rogue wild rabbit that was in amongst the parsnips. He wasn't entirely sure if Joseph was just winding him up when giving him rabbit-catching instructions, but he did as he was told anyway, even though he had no desire to catch the rabid-looking thing. It wasn't exactly a cute Watership Down bunny.

Tilly's mum, Lillian, was sitting at the large table, making a white dreamcatcher with her thin, wrinkly hands. Her big dark eyes rolled up to glance his way. 'Hello, Rory. Have you come to help me, son?'

He smiled warmly. 'I wouldn't know where to start.'

She gestured at the large box at the other end of the table. 'You can start by helping me pack this lot away and getting the casserole out of the oven. Wash your hands. You can sit with us tonight.'

Jamie came in before Rory had a chance to decline the offer. The Sheridans were doing so much for him already by giving him a job and a roof over his head. He didn't want to impose on their family time.

'Nan, have a word with Tills. She keeps trying to get me to walk Robyn home every time she comes in the shop to pick up Pepper Pot Farm's produce order. It's getting embarrassing now.'

Lillian moved his floppy dark hair from his forehead and kissed his temple. 'Carrying the girl's groceries home is the gentlemanly thing to do, Jamie. Isn't that right, Rory? You tell him.'

Jamie's button nose twitched in annoyance as he approached Rory at the sink to start washing his hands. 'She doesn't even like me.'

'Yes, she does,' said Tilly, entering and picking up her mum's craft box.

Jamie huffed as he looked over his shoulder, dripping water down Rory's jeans. 'She has a boyfriend, you know.'

Tilly's voice echoed from the hallway where she had taken the box. 'She and Zac Preston haven't been going out for two months. He wasn't even at her birthday party, in case you didn't notice.' She walked back in and started to help her mum lay the table ready for dinner. 'Why do you think she comes to the shop once a week instead of her gran? Josephine always picked up the weekly fruit and veg.'

Jamie tutted whilst drying his hands. 'Josephine Walker is about a hundred years old. I don't suppose she can carry much anymore.'

Bobby Sheridan opened the back door. 'Don't let Josephine hear you say she's one hundred. She'll hex you or something.' He laughed, taking off his coat and throwing it at Tilly.

39

'Oi!' Tilly took his coat to the hallway. 'You can let her read your palm, Jamie. She'll soon tell you if you're meant to end up with Robyn.'

Jamie blushed, which made Rory grin. 'I'm not going out with Robyn. She's just a kid.'

Tilly scoffed. 'She's one year younger than you. You went to her fourteenth birthday party.'

Jamie flapped his hands. 'Why is everyone so interested in my love life? Worry about yourselves. When was the last time you spoke to your husband, Uncle Bob?'

Bobby frowned. 'This morning, thank you very much.'

Tilly glanced up from the cutlery at Rory. 'Bob's better half lives in Ohio.'

'America?'

A few nods came his way.

'He has a business to run out there,' explained Bobby.

Tilly slid her body past Rory to grab some plates from behind him. 'Rex comes here for the summer, and our Bob goes out there in January.'

'That's the only time you see each other?' asked Rory, almost dancing with Tilly as she continued to manoeuvre around him. He desperately tried to ignore the tingling sensation fizzing in his stomach every time she grazed his body.

'We talk every day,' said Bobby, smiling widely, seeming completely happy with his long-distance relationship. 'He's going to move here once he retires. That's our plan.'

'Something smells good, Lillian,' said Joseph, standing in the doorway.

'Casserole.' She smiled warmly as her husband bent to kiss her cheek.

Joseph glanced over at Rory.

'Rory's staying for dinner tonight.' Lillian guided Rory to a chair and shoved him down before he had a chance to get out of the situation.

Joseph patted him on the shoulder as he passed him by.

'You wash your hands, Joseph,' she added.

He raised them in the air over the sink. 'I'm doing that right now.'

Jamie brought over a loaf of pumpkin seed bread and plonked it down in the middle of the table.

'Do you need a hand?' asked Rory, feeling lost in amongst the family hustle and bustle around him.

Lillian gave him a stern glare. 'You sit there, son. You've been working hard all day.'

Jamie huffed. 'So have I, Nan.'

'Aw, but you're young, Jamie lad,' said Joseph.

Bobby laughed. 'Rory's not an old man. How old are you, Rory?'

'Forty-nine.'

'See. He's only three years younger than me.'

'And you're not doing much to help either,' said Jamie, flicking a pumpkin seed at him.

'Stop that now,' said Lillian, moving Jamie away from the bread.'

'Someone's phone is ringing,' called out Tilly, looking out into the hallway.

'It's probably Bob's. Nobody else bothers with phones around here,' said Lillian, looking out towards the noise.

'Erm, I do,' said Jamie, fetching glasses over from the draining board. 'I'm just never allowed on it.'

'You're always on it,' scoffed Tilly.

Jamie patted his chest. 'I'm the one who keeps this farm's website up to date. That's what you see me doing on my phone.'

'Sure,' they all sung out, making Rory laugh.

Tilly placed the casserole on the table and threw the tea towel she was holding over towards the sink. 'Bob, come on. Dinner's ready.'

Bobby came back into the kitchen with his face staring at his phone. 'This is the Paul Newman lookalike I was telling you about.' He turned his phone to face Rory.

Rory pulled his head back and awkwardly waved at the red-bearded man in the phone grinning widely at him.

'You do have a touch of him about you,' said Rex.

Tilly placed her head in between Rory and the phone. 'Leave him alone, Rex. He's about to have his dinner.'

'I'm joining you,' said Rex, and with that Bobby propped his husband up by a jug of water.

Rory watched as Lillian engaged in a conversation with the phone whilst Bobby served himself dinner, Joseph cut some bread, and Tilly placed a large dish of roast potatoes on the table.

How lovely to be part of a happy family it must be. Look at them. Smiling, chatting, no fights, no one's drunk. Everyone looks relaxed in each other's company. I wish I had a family like this when I was growing up. Hell, I wish I had a family like this now. Aunt Jean would be yelling at her boyfriend right about now, and he would smash something. I'm surprised we had any crockery left the way those two went at it. Dad was never home for dinner. His usually went to the dog. So did mine sometimes, and for no reason.

Rory could see as clear as day the time when his step-mum had placed his dinner in front of him, waited for him to take his first bite, then swiped the plate away and tipped the contents into the dog's bowl. Her children had laughed, and he was told to sit on the floor by the dog until his dad came home from the pub. He knew if he moved, she would take her slipper to him, so he stayed there till gone midnight and then quietly went to bed when he heard his father fall in the door.

Jamie turned to him, showing his own phone. 'Look. Robyn sent me this text.'

Rory read the thank you message and nodded.

Jamie looked flustered as he swiped one hand through his mop of hair. 'What am I supposed to do about that?'

'Erm, nothing. She's just saying thanks for helping her home with the food. You could say, you're welcome, or something similar.'

'But then she might text back.'

Rory grinned as he nodded. 'Aye, she might.'

Jamie's shoulders slumped. He was clearly a fish out of water and didn't seem to care if Rory could see that. 'Then what?'

'Well now, that depends on whether you like the girl or not.' Rory watched the young lad bite down on his lip and shrug.

A spoonful of potatoes landed on his plate followed by a big smile from Tilly. He turned back to the dazed teenager at his side. 'Hey, if you like a girl, you've got to talk to her. It's as simple as that.'

Jamie whispered, 'It doesn't feel simple.'

Rory leaned closer to him. 'Women are complicated creatures, that's why, but you stick to the basics of idle chit-chat, and go from there.' He glanced up to see Tilly's raised brow and flashed her his best smile. He wasn't sure about the Paul Newman reference, but he did know that he had a smile about him that women seemed to like.

Joseph lowered the forkful of food he was about to eat. 'Oh, I got a call earlier from Nik down at Shine. There's a man he wants us to house for three days next week. Some hold-up with a hostel. I said we would. We've got two empty cottages, and like I said, it's only for three days.'

'Aw, that's okay, love. That won't be any trouble for us.' Lillian smiled over at her husband.

'Does this one look like anyone famous?' asked Rex.

Joseph chuckled, swallowing his food. 'I don't know what he looks like.'

'Didn't Nik give you any details?' asked Bobby, grinning at Rex.

'Of course he gives me details. He has to. It's part of his job, but he doesn't tell me what people look like. Where's the relevance in that? I do know the man's name though, if that helps feed your curiosity. It's Benny Tucker, but he likes to be called Tuck.'

Rory was grateful he didn't have any food in his mouth at that particular moment, because he would have choked or spat it across the table. He silently swore and made sure he didn't show any expression that could reveal exactly what he was thinking.

Benny Tucker, of all people, the lowlife, scummy, piece of shite. If he so much as looks sideways at Tilly, I'll rip his throat out, so help me God.

6

Tilly

Tall, slightly hunched, gaunt face, long rusty hair. Can't think of any Hollywood hunk he looks like. Rex will be disappointed when I tell him. I wonder if this man will ever buy anything. He's been lurking by the sweets for ages. There's not that much choice. I'm starting to feel a bit uncomfortable, and I'm never uncomfortable with people in my shop. I wish he would just leave. Okay, here he comes. Act natural.

'Hello, you must be Tuck. I'm Tilly, Joseph's daughter.'

Tuck produced a thin-lipped smile that didn't quite reach his green eyes. He offered his hand, and Tilly gripped his bony fingers. 'He's a good man, your dad. Putting me up and that. So, Tilly, you run this place, do ya?'

Strong London accent, seems friendly enough, still smiling at me, and yet, something feels off. I shouldn't judge a book by its cover, even if that cover does look like a knocked-off copy found out the back of a dark, seedy establishment that has an alleyway where the gutters are filled with blood. I've got to stop reading gory murder mysteries and go back to my nice cosies.

'Yep, just me, while everyone works the farm.'

He bobbed his head like one of those car toys as he glanced around. 'Not a bad little job.' He turned back and there was an odd gleam in his eyes that lasted all but a second. 'Nice gaff.'

'Thank you. I like it.'

'Don't suppose you get many punters round here though. Not exactly on the high street, are ya.'

Okay, so he likes small talk. I guess he's not so bad after all. He's clearly trying to make friends with me. I guess he probably feels a bit awkward being dumped here on us, and he's a long way from home. I would want a friend if I were in his position.

'Oh, we still do all right. We're handy for the locals. Plus, I make some fresh bread every morning, so that keeps them coming back.'

His smile widened. 'Smart move, young lady.'

Tilly laughed. 'Young lady. I'm probably older than you.'

'I'm thirty-nine, and that's the number I say every year. Keeps me where I want to be.'

He has a sense of humour. He's actually quite funny, not like that last man who stayed over for a couple of days after a mix-up with his hostel. I'll never forget him. Who was that actor who played Norman Bates? Oh, flipping heck, I can't remember now. I do remember not wanting to take a shower all the time he was here. Paranoid much. He did look so creepy though. I bet he doesn't make friends easily, but then I guess you wouldn't if you looked like a shower killer.

Tuck gestured towards the back of the shop. 'Blimey, I just had a thought. You must get up at the crack of dawn. That's what bakers do, right?'

Tilly followed his eyes whilst nodding. 'Hmm, very early. Four o'clock.'

His face was filled with admiration as he looked back. 'Cor, if I had to get up that early every day, I'd be asleep by dinnertime.'

'I do go to bed early. I'm knocked out till morning.'

'That would be me too. I do like my sleep. Heavy sleeper I am.'

'Me too.'

Tuck leaned on the counter, smiling directly into her eyes. 'It's always good to have things in common when making new friends, don't you think?'

Tilly slumped down onto her spongy chair behind the big old grey till that sat between her and her new customer, who still hadn't bought anything.

'So, we're friends now, are we, Tuck?'

He straightened and shrugged, flapping his arms widely. 'Why not?' He flashed a cheeky grin that was lopsided and made his mouth look drunk. 'I'm always up for making new mates, me. I think it comes from feeling so lonely when banged up, ya know? You don't get many friends inside, love.'

A pang of sadness hit her heart. There she was judging him in the beginning, thinking the worst, when all the time he was just another lonely soul out there in the world. 'I guess when you put it like that.' Her thoughts turned to Rory. Was that how he felt? Friendless and alone. 'Well, we're a friendly bunch here in Pepper Bay, so you'll be all right here with us, Tuck.'

'Aww, that's sweet of ya, babe. I like it here already, truth be told.'

'Have you just arrived?'

'About half hour ago. Your dad showed me where I'll be staying and then mentioned this place, so I thought I'd check it out.'

'You've been checking out the chocolate for ages.'

Tuck shook his head whilst frowning with disappointment. 'I've got such a sweet tooth, Tilly, but I haven't got any money for a few days. I guess I've just been tormenting myself by looking. Ah well, never mind, eh.'

Oh God, why do I feel so bad now? It's just a bar of chocolate. Hardly going to break the bank. I'll let him have one as a welcome-to-the-neighbourhood treat.

She walked over to the sweets and picked out a small bar of Dairy Milk and shoved it into his hand. 'From me to you, just to say welcome.'

He stared down at the bar of chocolate as if someone had just handed him a winning lottery ticket. 'Oh wow! Thanks, babe. I can't believe your kindness. I owe ya one.'

She waved his comment away, feeling rather pleased with herself. 'You don't owe me anything. That's what friends do, right?'

He took her hand and kissed her knuckles, which did make her feel slightly uncomfortable, although she wasn't sure why. He was smiling, being friendly, and thanking her. That was all.

'You're a mate alright, Tilly Sheridan. It is Sheridan, ain't it? You've not got an old man upstairs, have ya?'

She giggled at his waggling eyebrows. 'No. It's just me here.'

'Ah, no. Surely not. You live upstairs by yourself? Well, there's something very wrong with this world when a beautiful woman like yourself is on her lonesome.'

'Oh, stop with the mush.'

'Oi, I'm not talking cobblers. I'm just saying it how it is. So, what time do you close up around here? Early, I'm guessing. I can't see many trodding down that dirt track when it gets dark.'

'I close at half four every evening. It has always been quiet after that time, so I learnt to shut up shop at that time years ago.'

Tuck nodded whilst looking up at the ceiling above the counter. 'Makes sense.' His green eyes casually rolled her way. 'You're a smart lady, you. Good business sense. Hopefully, I'll get a good job soon. Sort me out for a while.'

'Are you hoping to stay here on the Isle of Wight?'

'Nah. No offence. It's a nice place and that, but it's more of a stopover for me. Nik brought me here for a bit. He reckons it'll be good for me.'

Nik thinks the island will be good for everyone. So far, no one's really taken to our place, and this man definitely doesn't look the farming type. He would, however, look right at home in an episode of Only Fools and Horses. Oh, God, I better not laugh.

'Well, you never know. Have you got any jobs lined up at all yet?'

The corner of his mouth tugged. 'I'm thinking there's one of interest.'

'Sounds like a start.'

'Yeah, it does.'

'I hope the job works out for you.'

His mouth twitched into a smile. 'So do I, love.'

She went to say something else but stopped when the shop door opened and Rory walked in. She watched him stand still for a second as his eyes met with Tuck.

What's wrong with him? Why isn't he his usual smiley self? Why is he looking at Tuck like that. The last time two men eyed each other that way was because they were a Shark and a Jet. Don't tell me these two know each other.

Tuck moved his face first. 'Bloody hell, if it ain't Murphy. What you doing here, mate?'

Rory seemed to hesitate. 'Working.'

Tuck looked amused, but Tilly only got a glance of that expression, as he turned his back on her. 'It's been a long time, mate. When did you get out?'

Rory's face was flat, bearing only a hint of a forced smile. 'Not that long ago.' He raised his cheekbones a bit more. 'Nik from Shine brought me here. Brought you here too, I guess. Do you want to catch up, Benny boy?' He dropped what little smile he had been holding on to, and his eyes remained pretty much lifeless, which was a whole new look to Tilly.

'Yeah, alright,' said Tuck.

Rory's face didn't change. 'Outside.'

Flipping heck, it sounds like he's asking him outside for a fight. Why is he using that tone? Are they friends or not? I should say something?

'Rory?'

His eyes rolled over Tuck's right shoulder and softened, offering some sort of normality. 'Hey, Tilly. I'm just going to catch up with my old friend here. I'll see you later.'

She watched him open the door, and his eyes went back to shark-mode as Tuck walked towards him.

Tuck glanced back her way. 'Cheers for the chocolate, love.'

Tilly smiled weakly as they left. She didn't like the nervous stirring she could feel in her gut.

What the hell was that all about?

7

Rory

Rory turned his head so sharply towards Tuck, he could have pulled a muscle. 'You touch her, and I'll kill ya.'

Tuck raised his hands as though he wasn't trying to offend. He was laughing as he made his way along the path that led to their cottages. 'You get first dibs, I get it, mate.'

With two big strides, Rory joined his side. 'That's not what I meant and you know it.'

Tuck stopped walking and twisted his nose in disgust. 'Oi, I'm not some pervert, ya know.'

'I know exactly what you are. You're not opposed to smacking someone in the mouth if they get in the way of your job, woman or no woman.'

'Cheers, mate. Make me sound like a monster, why don't ya.' Tuck turned to walk away.

Rory tugged his arm, stopping him along the track. 'I'm warning you, Tuck.'

'I thought you were some sort of saint nowadays. The last time I checked, you weren't going around threatening anyone anymore. The old Rory Murphy back, is he?'

'You hurt this family and you'll find out.'

Tuck laughed and carried on walking. 'What is up with you? I'm here for three days. I plan to sit back, put my feet up, and if I get the urge to steal anything, I'll grab an apple off one of those trees up there.' He gestured towards the orchard. 'If that's alright with you. It's not like there's anything else to nick around here.'

Oh really, is that a fact? You think I'm bloody stupid, don't you, Benny boy?

Rory pointed backwards. 'Did you just case the shop?'

'Not intentionally, but you know, old habits, and that.'

'That's what I'm worried about.'

'I'm not going to do anything, alright.'

'You'd better not, Tuck. Not this place. Not this family, ya hear?'

'I hear ya. Blimey, you're no fun anymore, Murphy. You used to be a right laugh when we were inside.'

'That was years ago. I haven't been that person you knew for a long time, and I haven't seen you in eleven years, so don't think you know me anymore, because you don't.'

'That's alright, mate. We all change over the years.'

Rory arched an eyebrow. 'Why do I get the feeling you haven't?'

Tuck shrugged, smiling as he entered his temporary accommodation. 'Beats me.'

There was so much left of the day, and there were two more days until Tuck left.

Rory entered his own home and stared at the wall between him and the man from his past.

He won't try anything today, nor tomorrow. It'll be the last day. When he knows he's leaving. Probably. Unless he doesn't plan to go back with Nik. If he's thinking that way, he's likely to make his move the last night and then do a runner. Okay, how to play this. I can't warn anyone. They'll just say I'm making assumptions, and Tuck's just trying to rebuild his life, and I should be giving him a chance, blah, blah, blah. I wonder if there are any extra locks in the shed. That shop isn't secure at all. I bet his eyes lit up as soon as he looked it over. How can I get Tilly to agree to extra security without raising suspicion? I wonder how much info he got out of her. I need to talk to her. Have a proper look round. See what angle he's going to take.

Rory closed his front door quietly and made his way back to the shop.

'Why were you acting weird earlier?' was the thing out of Tilly's mouth as soon as he entered the premises.

He rocked the door back and forward, eyeing it up and down as though something was wrong with the hinges. He was stalling for time whilst plotting how to get another lock on the old cottage-style door.

'Rory?'

I have to say something. I can feel her eyes boring into the back of my neck. She's already suspicious. Maybe that's not entirely a bad thing. It might keep her on her toes around here. She's too friendly. I bet she told Tuck what time she gets up, what time she goes to bed, that she lives here alone. Oh, Tilly love. What did you tell that man? He wasn't being friendly. He was working you. Tuck only needs twenty minutes with someone to get their passwords. He's got skills, I'll give him that.

'Rory?'

Come on, Murphy, wake up. Box clever.

'Hmm?'

She came from behind the counter to stand at his side. 'Are you going to tell me?'

He kept his eyes on the door, pretending to look interested in the lock. 'Tell you what?'

'You and Tuck.'

'Oh, him, yeah. I knew him in London. Seen him around. You know. Then he was in the same prison as me a couple of times. Not much to tell.'

Her arms were folded and her lips pursed. He knew the body language. He knew the look. He glanced up at the chunky doorframe above his head.

'I think I'm going to have to put another lock on this door, Tilly love.' He chanced a glance her way. 'To help take the weight off the hinges.'

It was possible he had distracted her mind for a moment, as her eyes had stopped boring into him and were now staring at the door.

'What's wrong with the hinges?'

There had been many times in Rory's life when he had to blag his way out of trouble, throw out some spiel, or simply talk utter crap, winging his way through a conversation as slick as a conman and as shrewd as a predator, but today wasn't one of them. He fumbled over any words that managed to fly through his mind and cleared his throat for so long, anyone listening would have thought he needed some honey and lemon.

'The door is old,' he managed, swallowing hard and wondering when he had lost his ability to lie. 'So, I'm thinking that if I add another lock, it will help alleviate the weight caused by the frail structure and distribute the mass, creating balance and more sturdiness in the framework.'

What the feck am I talking about?

Confusion wasn't just in her eyes. He quickly rolled his away and nodded. 'Yeah, that should do the trick. I'll go see if there is a spare in the shed.'

'Erm, wait a minute.'

Ah crap!

'I'm pretty sure there is nothing wrong with that door.' She looked pretty sure, like some sort of shop door expert.

'It's old. It's weak.'

She arched an eyebrow, with sarcasm written all over her face. 'It's fine and has been for years. Haven't you got any work to do today? Is that why you're here faffing about with my door? Are you trying to create jobs now?'

Okay, so she's not stupid when it comes to me. Now what? Think. Think. Change tactics.

He closed the door and took a step towards her. She loosened the grip she had on herself and slumped back to rest on one heel. A twitch hit the corner of his mouth at how nervous she suddenly looked being so close to him.

She's flustered. Don't laugh. God, she looks cute. She's actually blushing. Now, there's a sight. Confident, chatty Tilly Sheridan, all quiet and tense. I want to grab those dungarees of hers and tug her forward into my arms. I could. I won't. I shouldn't, but oh, I could. I really could.

His eyes darkened as he stared down at her mouth.

Tilly swallowed hard and stumbled over her own foot as she attempted to move backwards a step.

Rory grabbed her elbows and moved into her space. He tilted his head and lowered his face towards hers.

She swallowed again and opened her mouth. 'Why are you really here?'

Her words jolted him out of the trance he had found himself in. He needed to walk away, to concentrate on his task, but the goalposts had been moved, and now he was a little lost. He leaned closer to her mouth and held back a smile. 'I came in to get some custard creams.' His voice was barely a whisper.

Her shaky breath noticeably caught in her throat. 'Custard creams?'

'Aye. I've got a fancy.'

And it's not the biscuits, Tilly Sheridan. You have no idea how much willpower it's taking me right now to not kiss you. Christ, Tilly, you've got my stomach in knots here.

As though someone had just smacked her straight in the jaw, she jumped back and turned sharply, heading for the biscuits, leaving his building fizz to fall as flat as left-open cola.

He sighed inwardly at his pathetic attempt to weaken her knees.

Ah, Rory, you eejit. You couldn't tease a donkey with a carrot. What are you like? You're an old man now, ya know. Silly bugger, and where the feck did custard creams come from? Where's my mind at? I should have got my head straight way before I came in here. I needed a better plan. What did I have? Not a lot, that's what. Dodgy hinges and distraction by some weird attempt at flirting. That sure as hell wasn't flirting. Anyway, it backfired, because I'm the one feeling nervous and tense now. This woman's definitely under my skin already. I should have just kissed her. No, I shouldn't have. I'm glad I didn't. Argh! I'm going to mess this up, I know I am, and now I've got Benny bloody Tuck to deal with. Why me? Why can't I just have a normal life for once? Is it too much to ask for? I guess, I'm jinxed or something. That's got to be it.

Tilly placed the packet of biscuits on the counter and entered the amount in the till, and Rory pulled out his wallet and paid for the item he didn't actually want. Her eyes casually rolled up, waiting, and he was pretty sure his heart just skipped a beat, maybe even two.

There was only so long people could stare at each other before the atmosphere turned awkward, and he knew he had just maxed out his time.

He raised the custard creams in the air and gestured towards the door with his head. 'I'll be off now then.'

She smiled tightly. 'Enjoy your biscuits.'

'Aye,' he mumbled to himself, feeling agitated and slightly fed up. He gave the door the death glare on his way out and finally exhaled all the frustrated energy he had built up inside the shop.

Okay. Plan B.

8

Tilly

It was ten o'clock at night, and Tilly was happily snuggled in bed, having not long turned the heating off. She placed her reading glasses on the cream bedside cabinet and turned off her kindle. She took a small sip from the bottle of water sitting there and switched off her lamp.

Whilst smiling, feeling grateful for her bed, something tapped her window, making her jump. Deciding to ignore whatever had just blown by in the wind, she closed her weary eyes. A beat later, and a splatter of something sounding a lot like grit hit her window, causing her to jolt upright.

What the hell was that?

Another clunk filled her bedroom, and that was enough of that. She got up and looked out of the window, frowning down at the figure standing in her back garden.

A hand waved up at her.

It was dark outside, and there weren't any garden lights to give a better picture as to who was out there, obviously throwing stones at her window.

The hand was now flapping and gesturing for her to open the window, so she did.

'Tilly, will you open the back door, for the love of God, woman. I'm freezing out here,' said Rory, looking up.

'Rory, what are you doing out there?' She had no idea why she was whispering. It wasn't as though she would wake the neighbours.

'Waiting for you to let me in.' His jaw was clenched and his arms wrapped around his chest.

'Why haven't you got a coat?'

He huffed loudly. 'Will you let me in.'

She closed the window, wrapped her dressing gown over her shorts and vest top pyjamas, and made her way into the kitchen downstairs.

Rory rushed inside. 'Jesus, it's cold tonight.'

She locked the door behind him, wondering why he was looking over her shoulder to check. 'What's wrong? Why are you here so late? I was just about to go to sleep.'

'Aye, I know your schedule. I'm just going to stay here tonight, if it's all right with you.'

She knew he wasn't asking, and she also got the feeling he wasn't inviting himself to her room. 'Rory, what's going on?'

He moved over to the kettle and gave it a rattle. 'Do you mind?' he asked, gesturing to the tap.

'Why not. Just come on in and make yourself at home.' Her face fell flat. 'Tell me what you're doing, and don't say making a cup of tea.'

He turned away from the kettle. 'You're going to think I'm nuts.'

'Already there. So, let's try again. What's going on? You've been acting weird for a few days now, ever since Tuck arrived, and now you want to suddenly sleep with me?'

His eyes widened.

'I mean, sleep here,' she quickly corrected. She waggled her finger at him. 'You'd better start talking, Rory Murphy, and yes I would use your middle name if I knew it.'

He grinned and butterflies decided to also rock up at ten o'clock at night to join the party.

'Okay, but I don't want you to get scared...'

'Oh, that's a great start.'

'Hey, Tilly, you're not to feel scared, okay? You're safe, I promise.'

'You can't say you don't want me to be scared and then expect me not to automatically be scared. I thought you had studied psychology.'

'I didn't know you would feel scared straight away.'

'Of course I'm scared. You're throwing stones at my window, coming into my home late at night, telling me you're staying here, but not even wanting to get in my bed, and the first explanation you give starts with me being told not to be scared.'

'Well, when you put it like that...'

'Can you actually get to the point tonight? Anytime soon would be good.'

Rory turned to switch the kettle on and obviously knew better than to offer her a cup at that particular moment in time. 'I'm not saying it will happen, but if I had to bet on it, then I would say it was going to happen tonight.'

Tilly grabbed his arm, took a split second to admire the muscles she could feel, and then forced him to turn around to face her. 'What's happening tonight, Rory?'

'I think that Tuck will try to rob this place tonight.'

A sudden sickly churning filled her stomach. She stepped back, and he caught her arms, holding her close to him.

'Hey,' he said softly. 'I'll not let that happen.'

Taking a moment to process the information, and to stop staring at his solid chest, she moved out of his reach to sit at the table.

Rory pulled out a chair next to her, sat down, and reached out to hold her hands. 'It's going to be okay, Tilly love. I'm just going to stay awake down here for the night, just in case. That's all.'

She rolled her eyes up. 'But… Tuck is leaving with Nik in the morning. Surely he wouldn't be stupid enough to rob the shop before he leaves. He would know all eyes would turn to him.'

'I'm not sure he has any intention of going with Nik tomorrow. I'm thinking he'll do the job and disappear.'

'The police will just wait for him at the ferry.'

'Yeah, well, he never was the brightest star.'

Tilly could feel her anger bubbling as it dawned on her that Tuck had only pretended to be her friend. 'I was nice to him. I even gave him a free bar of chocolate.'

'Hey, don't feel too mugged off. He's been in this game for years.'

The kettle had boiled, but Tilly tightened her grip on his fingers as he went to slip away. He stayed, looking her in the eyes.

'I could be wrong, you know, Tilly. He might not come.'

'But your instincts told you that he would.'

'Aye.'

She sighed deeply and glanced around the kitchen. 'Looks like we're in for a long night then.'

Rory breathed out a laugh. 'Yeah, me, not you.'

'I'm not leaving you down here on your own all night.'

He flashed her a smile, and her stomach flipped up to her throat. 'You can go back to bed now, Tilly love. I'll be fine down here by myself. Just turn the heating on a bit, will you?'

'But what if he breaks in?' She could see he was mulling over his words, and it was irritating her. She wanted him to just be straight with her, not handle her with kid gloves.

'I'll just scare him off,' he said, letting go of one of her hands to wave the air.

There was a coldness in her vacant hand already. She glanced down at her fingers, hoping his would return soon. 'That's not good enough, Rory. We need a solid plan.'

'I was just going to punch him in the face.'

'I'm being serious.'

'So am I.'

'And then you'll get arrested too, and you're not going back to prison. You can't.' She realised she was gripping his hand a bit too tightly when his fingers started to wiggle free.

'Okay. We'll have a proper plan. Just give my hand back some blood now.'

She let go and watched him stand, leaving even more space between them, which she wasn't keen on. Now, she wanted to hold more than just his hand. She wanted to wrap herself around him and hold him as close as possible.

Oh God, really? Why? I need to get my head in the game. I could be robbed tonight by that conning, conniving, crooked...

'We'll call the police. They can come and wait with us, and we'll catch him together.'

Rory smiled warmly. 'They won't sit with us, Tilly love. We have no proof a crime is about to be committed. They're not going to go on my hunch.'

'Well then, as soon as he fiddles with the locks, I'm calling the police.'

'Okay, but you can do that from upstairs. Do you have a door you can lock up there?'

'Only the bathroom.'

He tutted and shook his head. 'The security around here is terrible, you know that?'

'So that's why you wanted to put an extra lock on the front door.'

Ignoring that, he glanced up at the ceiling. 'I've already checked out this place, but enlighten me. Do you have any alarms or cameras hidden about that I've not seen?'

She shook her head, feeling slightly stupid all of a sudden. 'We've never needed anything like that around here. We've been here forever, and we've never been robbed. Even back when this place was just a post office, it was left alone.'

'And is your safe upstairs? I need to know where he might snoop.'

She shook her head and glanced out to the shopfront. 'No, it's under the till.'

'Under the till? Are you kidding me?'

'Well, what's wrong with that? It's not as though I have the crown jewels in there. Just the weeks' takings.'

He shook his head, huffing to himself. 'And I bet you go to the bank at the same time on the same day every week.'

She gave a half-shrug, not liking the fact that he was implying she was thick.

'Ah, Tilly love, what am I going to do with you? Starting tomorrow, I'm going to add some security to this place. You're a big fat target here, you know.'

She watched him walk over to the light switch and turn it off. 'Do we have to sit in the dark?'

'Aye, if we want to catch him red-handed.'

'But if we left the lights on all night, he'll know someone is up, and he won't try anything.'

'Ah, well, now, that doesn't always deter Benny boy. Anyway, if he is going to rob this place, then it proves he shouldn't be getting help from the likes of Shine. He's playing the system, as many do, and I don't want Nik getting hurt in the crossfire. I don't want you getting hurt either, so will you go upstairs now, please?'

Tilly shook her head. 'No, I want to stay with you.'

'I can't have you here with me, Tilly love. I need to know you're out of harm's way so I can think clearly when dealing with him. He's not the type to go down without a fight.'

She didn't want to put too much thought into it, as she didn't want to talk herself out of her actions, so she quickly stepped forward and swung her arms around his waist and held on.

It obviously took him by surprise, as he stilled for a moment, but then his arms came around her and pulled her closer.

She could feel his mouth pressing down on her head, and his breath seeping into her hair.

'Hey, Tilly, what's all this?' he whispered.

She felt no shame in telling him what was running through her mind. 'I'm scared you might get hurt.' Her voice was muffled by his grey sweatshirt, but she was pretty sure he still heard her.

He pulled her back to look at her face, and just for a moment they simply stared at each other.

His hand came up and gently placed her hair behind her ear. 'I'll be okay. I promise.'

'What if he has a weapon?'

'Then, I'll use one too.'

'But you don't have any weapons.'

Rory grinned. 'Look around you, Tilly. We're surrounded by weapons.'

She glanced sideways, thinking Tuck could be bopped on the head by the kettle.

That would work.

'Throw the kettle at him.'

Rory breathed out a laugh. 'I was thinking of throwing a tin of spaghetti hoops at his head, but I like your style.'

She gently squeezed his arm and groaned. 'This isn't the time for jokes.'

He grinned widely. 'Oh, so you actually want me to take him out with a kettle, do you? There's a coldness to you I've not seen before, Tilly Sheridan.'

'Speaking of cold, let me turn the heating back on.' She moved away, missing his touch already, and sorted the temperature dial. 'Rory, come and sit over here.' She waved him towards a small floral sofa that was squashed in the corner of the room, over by the toilet.

It was a snug fit, but neither of them seemed to mind. He placed his arm around her as though it was the most natural thing to do, and she snuggled closer to his chest.

'Why do you have a sofa in the kitchen, Tilly?'

'Sometimes my back aches working down here, so I sit here when I have my lunch. It's more comfortable than the chairs.'

'Aye, I have to agree there.'

She could feel his mouth on her head again.

'Tilly love, you haven't made me a promise yet.'

'What's that?'

'Promise me that if anything happens here tonight, you'll go straight upstairs, lock yourself in the bathroom, and call the police and not come out until they arrive, no matter what you hear down here.'

Silence filled the air, only disturbed by one drip of water falling from the tap.

'I don't like the end of that statement, Rory.'

He lifted her away from him, and she could see how serious his eyes were. 'Can you just promise?'

It seemed the sensible thing to do. She agreed, and he breathed out a heavy sigh before placing her back against his chest.

I hope Tuck has reformed. I really do, for all our sakes. I can't even call Dad or Bobby. They'd come straight here, then more people could get hurt. Rory wouldn't be here if he didn't think Tuck was capable of... God, what is that man capable of? What other crimes has he committed in the past?

'Patrick.'

Tilly lost her train of thought. 'What?'

'My middle name is Patrick.'

She smiled to herself. 'Your name is very Irish.'

'My parents were very Irish.'

She snorted out a laugh, then had a sudden thought. 'My parents didn't really opt for a theme when naming us. Well, apart from our middle names, sort of, I guess.'

'What's your middle name?'

She bit her lip for a second, knowing he was going to laugh, as most people did.

'Oh, come on.' He chuckled. 'It can't be that bad.'

His chest was vibrating against her ear, so she sat up, wanting to look into those grey-blue eyes of his. They were happily twinkling her way as though he didn't have a care in the world, let alone the worry of coming face to face with a potential burglar and getting into a possible fight.

'Moon,' she told him, twisting her mouth to one side.

He arched an eyebrow. 'Matilda Moon. That's cute.'

'My mum thought so.'

'What's everyone called?'

'My eldest brother is Mitchum Rainbow, and the next one is Romeo River. Bobby is Roberto Dream, and my little sister was Luna Butterfly. We all got a butterfly tattoo done after she died.'

'Well, they're certainly different. So, where's your butterfly tatt then?'

66

She blushed, glad of the darkness, and glad he couldn't read minds, because just for a second she had visualised his fingertips stroking over her skin at that very spot. 'Lower back, just to the right.'

'I'll have to check that out one day.'

So, you were thinking the same thing.

She lowered her eyes whilst trying not to burst out into a huge smile. She went to speak, but he jolted upright, eyes focused on the doorway that led to the shop. His finger rested gently on her lips, and even though a man was attempting to break into her shop, she so wanted to kiss Rory's hand. Their eyes met and didn't move for a moment, and now she wanted to kiss more than his hand.

Rory slowly stood, taking her with him. 'You promised me.'

Oh God, I don't know what to do.

A flurry of fear raced through her heart, interrupting her breathing pattern.

'Go,' he whispered close to her mouth. 'Call the police. Tell them someone is in your shop.'

She nodded, struggling so hard to let her hand slip from his as he guided her to the door that led upstairs.

The lock on the bathroom door didn't seem as secure as it used to, but it was all she had to protect herself from Tuck. That and Rory. She quickly called the police and told them what was going on. The nearest police station was over in Sandly, so it wouldn't take them long to arrive, she hoped.

For some reason, curling up in the bath seemed like the place to be. She hugged her knees and prayed Rory wouldn't get hurt. Then, another thought flashed through her mind.

What if they're in it together? What if Rory sent me up here so that they can steal the lot? No. He wouldn't. Would he? I don't really know him. He could be fooling me, like

Tuck did. They've known each other for years. What if they planned this, and I'm sitting up here like an idiot? What if he has wormed his way into my heart just so he can worm his way into my petty cash? Oh, what am I thinking? All of my instincts say he's a good man. A changed man, but what do I really know?

She clambered out the bath and pressed her ear up against the door.

It's pretty quiet out there. Maybe I should take a peek. No, wait for the police. Be sensible. Oh, Luna, wait till I write about this to you. It could quite possibly be the most exciting letter I have ever written to you. Not sure exciting is the right word. I don't know what describes any of this night.

A loud crashing noise came from the shop, making Tilly jump. She squeezed herself closer to the door, willing herself not to open it for more details. There seemed to be a scuffle going on, that much was clear, but there weren't any other noises to indicate a fight was taking place. There was no screaming or shouting, no swearing or name-calling, absolutely nothing.

Oh, where the hell are the police?

Another loud bang rattled her insides.

What if they're throwing stuff around to scare me, making it seem as if they're fighting, when really they're laughing? Laughing at me. Look around you, Tilly, you're surrounded by weapons. What could I use? I'm not going to stand much of a chance against those two, but it'll give me great satisfaction to whack Rory around the head with something if he is down there laughing at me whilst stealing my stuff.

Her eyes drifted to the hairspray on the dresser.

That will definitely sting the eyes. Then I can kick him in the groin. That's one down. Oh flipping heck, why didn't I pay more attention when Bobby made me sit through his Jackie Chan films?

She looked around the bedroom for something that would hopefully knock Tuck all the way out, as she didn't want him getting back up either.

Oh, who am I trying to kid! I'm hardly one of Charlie's Angels. Mr Kipling's Angel Slice, that's about it for me.

Another crashing sound filled the air, and Tilly could take no more. She had to know what was going on. Was she being fooled, or worse, was Rory hurt?

She tiptoed downstairs and slipped into the darkness of the kitchen to grab the kettle.

The shop was a mess. There were rows of shelving knocked over, food items sprawled across the floor, and the till seemed to be missing.

She slid her hand down the wall and caught the light switch. The chaos of the shop was fully visible, revealing the two men grappling on the floor in amongst the cornflakes and those nasty porridge cereal bars that reminded her of hamster food.

Rory's head shot up to look at her, and Tuck got in a right hook that freed him from Rory's hold. He jumped up and propelled himself at Tilly.

She gasped and swung the kettle, catching his arm, but Tuck didn't flinch. He pushed her over the chest freezer, twisted her arm behind her back, and pinned her face to the glass. She could see fire in Rory's eyes as he approached.

'I'll break her arm,' Tuck told him, and Tilly believed him. Her arm was hurting so much already, and she really wished she'd had more faith in Rory and stayed in the bath.

Blood was dripping from his head and mouth, and she couldn't help but visualise vampires as pain ripped through her arm.

Rory stood still and pointed one finger at Tuck. 'Break her arm. I dare ya.'

What? What is he saying? This isn't the time for dares.

She was watching his eyes, but he was focused on Tuck's. There was an almost robot-look about Rory that she couldn't make out. He didn't seem human. His face was dead, and his eyes suddenly vacant. The only thing that made him seem alive was his shaky hands, but she was sure that was probably just his adrenaline, as he sure as hell didn't look one bit scared.

'I'm just gonna leave, alright?' said Tuck, sounding more how a human under those circumstances should sound.

Rory gave a slight shake of the head. 'Too late for that.'

What? No, it's not. Let him leave. What's wrong with you?

She felt Tuck's stale breath hit her cheek. 'Tell him to back off, babe.'

Rory's eyes were still on Tuck, and Tilly wasn't sure what she could say to snap him out of the Terminator mood he seemed to be in.

Tuck twisted her arm some more, causing her to cry out in pain.

I want to kill him.

She screamed at Rory, 'Hit him with the kettle.'

Tuck shot up as Rory threw himself forward, grabbed the kettle from the floor, swung it straight into Tuck's head, and rugby-tackled him to the floor.

Tilly straightened her sore arm just as sirens filled the air. She looked over at the window to see blue lights flashing and quickly ran to the door.

'Help… Inside,' she blurted out.

The police piled in whilst she inhaled the cold air before running back inside.

Rory and Tuck were on their fronts with their hands cuffed behind their backs.

'No, no,' she cried. 'Rory's not the robber. He is.' She pointed at Tuck, really wanting to kick him in the ribs. She squatted to Rory's side, placing her hand on his back. 'He's with me. He works here. He was helping to fight off the intruder.'

Joseph ran into the shop. 'Tilly. Tilly.' He froze on seeing the huddle on the floor. 'What the hell is going on?'

Tilly was so pleased to see her dad. Everything suddenly felt so much better. 'Dad. Tuck was robbing the place. We were trying to stop him. Tell them to untie Rory.'

One of the older officers looked up at her dad. 'He with you, Joseph?'

'Yeah, Brian. That's Rory Murphy, my farmhand. You can let him go.'

Officer *Brian* uncuffed Rory and helped him to stand.

Rory stumbled slightly, nodding at Joseph.

Tilly flung her arms around him, holding him as though her life depended on it. His arms felt weak as they came to rest around her.

'Tilly,' said Joseph, gesturing towards the doorway that led to upstairs. 'Take Rory and get him cleaned up. I'll deal with this.'

Tilly just caught a glimpse of Bobby running into the shop as she guided Rory upstairs.

9

Rory

The cool cloth on his head soothed more than his cut as his weary soul relaxed into Tilly's soft touch. She cleaned his busted lip, wiped away blood from his head wound, stripped him down to his black boxers, put his stained clothes on a cold cycle, and had him sitting in her bed with a cup of tea.

Her eyes had practically examined every inch of him when he stood in front of her in just his underwear. The pain from his fight was just starting to make itself known, which he was pleased about at that moment. He needed the distraction because her dilated pupils and slightly parted mouth were beckoning him. He was glad to hide parts of himself under the bed covers.

Ah, I'm aching now. I'm going to feel this in the morning. Christ, I'm feeling old right now.

'Here, let me look.' She removed the small tea towel from his head. 'That's dried up nicely, but I'm going to put butterfly stitches on it now, okay?'

He smiled softly and winced. 'Yes, miss.'

Tilly leaned over and stuck the small white strips over the wound. 'What a state you're in, Rory Patrick Murphy. There. That's better.'

'It's just a scratch. I've looked worse.'

'Hmm, I'm sure you have.' She handed over a couple of painkillers and a bottle of water.

The water dripped down his chin, due to his fat lip hurting when trying to drink. He tried not to laugh at himself. 'Oh, that was tricky.'

Tilly scribbled on a piece of paper and put it down on the tray she had placed on a chair by the bed.

'What you writing there, nurse?'

'Your medication times.'

His heart warmed as she briefly smiled his way. There was exhaustion in her eyes but it didn't stop the small twinkle that flashed his way. He saw her take a deep breath before she got up from the side of the bed, and a wave of guilt washed over him.

This is all my fault. I should have warned the Sheridans about Tuck, or at least told Nik. Her shop's a mess, she's shaken, I know, and Joseph will probably want me to leave too. I don't blame him if he does. It's his daughter who has been affected by ex-crims staying at the farm. They might put an end to the help they give now. People like Tuck don't exactly help the cause. I can't believe I nearly got arrested again, and because of him. My life has changed now. Someone needs to get that memo. I'm happy here on the farm with Tilly. Where would I go if I have to leave here? How will I feel about never seeing her again?

The little energy he did have was fading into the night. He wanted to hold her and tell her things he'd never said to another woman before. Confess all his secrets. The ones about her that he had stored in his heart.

Tilly rubbed her arm, attracting his attention.

'Are you in pain, Tilly love?'

She glanced over her shoulder. A feeble smile proved she was lying when she told him that she was fine.

He leant his head back against the pillow squashed against the dark-wood headboard, closed his eyes for a second, and took a silent, deep breath.

She was putting blood-stained tea towels into a plastic laundry basket when he glanced over.

'Tilly,' he said softly, stopping her from leaving the bedroom.

She slid the basket onto her hip. 'Hmm?'

'Come here, would you.'

Slowly, she walked over to him, the basket still firmly in place.

'Put that down a minute.' He patted the bed. 'Sit here a sec.'

She did as he instructed and slumped down to sit upon the quilt, rubbing her arm again.

'Take your dressing gown off. I want to look at your arm.'

He was half-expecting an argument, but she let the dressing gown fall down to her waist to reveal her vest top.

He was well aware that her spaghetti-strap top was the least amount of clothes he had seen her in. Her bare arms and top half of her chest caused him to still for a moment. Right there in front of him was pale, smooth skin that was within reach of his mouth. He swallowed hard and finally leaned forward, gently taking her arm to examine it for bruising. His finger started to lightly stroke around her shoulder. There were so many other parts of her that he wanted to run his finger lightly over. So much of her that he wanted to see. To taste. To have knowledge of. She was watching the swirling motion of his fingertip with him.

'It's just a bit sore, that's all.' Her voice was so quiet and deflated, it tore into his heart and burned the back of his eyes.

I want to make it right for you, Tilly. I want to take your pain away. I want to take this night away, except for this part where I get to hold you so close in bed.

He lowered his head to her shoulder, almost touching it with his lips. An invisible pull kept him from kissing her skin. He wasn't sure what it was holding him back. It was tormenting him, whatever it was. 'I'm so sorry about your arm, Tilly.'

'It wasn't your fault. It was mine. I should have listened to you and stayed upstairs.'

There was a croak in her wobbly voice. He couldn't bear it. The agitation stirring in his gut felt hot and acidic. 'You're not to blame. This could have all been avoided if I had just voiced my concerns to Nik or someone.' He lowered her arm and shifted towards her, wanting more of her. He had to hold off. She deserved better than the likes of him.

What a mess. What a great big bloody mess. I have to do something to ease her somehow.

'I need to leave, Tilly. I don't think I can stay here now.'

She jolted her head up and grabbed his hand with such force, he jumped slightly. 'What? No. You can't leave.'

She's digging her fingers in me. Does she even know? Do I even care?

'I can't stay. Look what I've done to your business, your family, you.'

'You haven't done anything, Rory. You saved my shop, and me.'

'But if I had just said…' A flutter hit his solar plexus.

Her fingers were gently resting on his mouth, just to the side of his busted lip. 'Shh! Lie back now.' Her voice was hushed and comforting, making him feel almost sedated. 'You're going nowhere. You're in my bed now.'

He closed his eyes as his head met with the soft pillow behind him. Her gentle fingers slowly reached along his hairline, sweeping his hair away from his forehead, soothing every part of him. His breathing settled, and his bruised and battered body relaxed.

A slow moan left his parted lips. 'Aw, Tilly, that feels so good.'

The warmth of her mouth pressed lightly against his cheek. He opened his eyes to see her smile affectionately at him. There were so many conversations in that one look.

'Rest now, Rory love,' she whispered. 'I'm just going to pop downstairs to find out what's going on. I'll be back in a minute.'

They remained staring at each other until she blinked first and moved away.

The sound of heavy footsteps trotted down the stairs, leaving him with a sudden lonely feeling.

Rory had spent most of his life feeling lonely. It wasn't an emotion that bothered him much, he was that used to it. It was simply a part of who he was, but this felt different. Tilly made the emptiness around him feel wider, bigger, more noticeable.

Rory love.

He smiled to himself, then winced and touched his lip. 'Ow!'

Dread to think what I'm going to look like in the morning. I'm going to have to go home in a bit, and the police probably want a statement. Nik will no doubt be here first thing. Bloody Benny Tucker. I want to smack him in the face again. God, I haven't had a fight in ten years. If I ever do see him again, I'm definitely going to break his arm. How far have I actually come if I can let someone get under my skin like that? Christ, when he touched Tilly, I was going back inside. Ain't that the truth.

He groaned as he shifted his weight. Without Tilly around, he felt more comfortable revealing his pain.

I hope she's not tidying up down there. That can wait till morning. I'll clear up the mess I made. Maybe I should go and check. Ah, she's going to have a right go if I get up. That's for sure.

He flopped back as footsteps were heading his way.

Tilly stood in the doorway, appearing to assess the situation. 'Did you get up?'

'No, miss. I haven't moved.' The touch of her hand upon his forehead was welcome. He closed his eyes again and silently sighed.

Where have you been all my life, Matilda Moon Sheridan? Why couldn't I have met you years ago? I don't suppose you would have looked twice at me back then. Not that man, but if I had grown up with someone like you around, maybe I would have stood a chance at knowing what love felt like. You make me think about love. You make me feel. I need to think about something else before I bloody well start crying. I don't cry. Feel like doing it though. See that, Tilly love, you really do make me feel.

'Dad's sorted everything, for now.' Her voice was quiet as though she didn't want to disturb him. 'The police have gone, but we have to go to the station and give statements tomorrow. Bobby's boarded up a broken window, and if you heard any banging, that was Dad fixing a temporary lock on the front door. I'll clear up in the morning.'

'We'll clear up in the morning.'

'Mum's been on the phone, wanting me to sleep up at the house tonight, but I said we'll be fine here, or would you prefer that?'

Hell no. I don't want to move out of your presence. Your bed is currently my favourite place in the world. And I like looking at you. I want to stay looking at you. I'll take that for as long as I can.

'I want to stay wherever you are, Tilly love, but if you feel safer up at the house, then I can go home.'

'I feel safe here with you.'

The bed dipped next to him, and Tilly slipped under the covers on what was clearly not her usual side of the bed, judging by everything on her nightstand next to him. She arched an eyebrow as she tossed her dressing gown towards the end of the bed. 'I'm not sleeping on the floor.'

He raised the good side of his mouth. 'I'm not complaining. I don't mind you bedding down with me for the night.'

'Good. Snuggle down lower then. Get comfortable. It's late, and I'm tired.'

He did as he was told and turned slightly to face her. She looked pale and worn out, and a wave of guilt hit him once again. 'Tilly, I'm sorry…'

'Please don't say sorry again, Rory. I'm too tired to keep going over this with you.'

He noticed a tear escape the corner of her eye. It rolled down her face and disappeared into the plump pillow.

'Hey.' He reached over and wiped her cheek. 'Don't cry, Tilly love. Please don't cry.'

'I'm okay. Just a bit exhausted, that's all.'

He raised his head and beckoned her closer. 'Come in for a cuddle. God knows I need one.'

There was no asking twice. She slid over, and he held her against him, ignoring the bruising in his ribs. Gently stroking her arm, he started to hum an Irish ditty that his dad used to sing when he'd come home drunk and happy.

10

Tilly

The colours of autumn filled Hope Park for the Sandly Harvest Festival. Rows of market stalls lined walkways, strewn with orange, red, and gold bunting. Bales of straw were used as seating in amongst scarecrows and bunches of corn. A large greying-white food and beer tent sat next to the food donations kiosk, and as it was such a glorious sunny day, the donkeys from the local donkey sanctuary were out in a sectioned-off area, happily being petted by children dressed as scarecrows, who were ready for the scarecrow fancy dress competition.

Tilly was standing behind Dreamcatcher Farm's wooden stall, handing over a paper bag filled with cooking apples to a couple of old ladies and learning all about the correct way to make an apple crumble. She smiled their way as they left, then glanced down the other end of the market barrow at Rory, who was talking to Jamie.

Jamie kept looking over at the walkway every few seconds as Rory whispered close to his ear. It seemed like a deep and meaningful conversation, because her nephew had his serious face on.

What are they whispering about. What's he looking at?

She looked over to see long strawberry-blonde hair and knew straight away it was Robyn who Jamie was glancing at.

Ah, now I see.

Robyn turned and smiled at Tilly. Her pale-lavender eyes twinkled as they rolled towards Jamie.

Tilly watched Jamie lower his head and turn back to Rory. *Wow, this is actually painful to watch. Was I that shy as a teenager? I can't remember. Probably was. Mind you, I can't say anything. I still have a funny turn every time I think about Rory coming out of my bathroom the morning after he stayed the night with me. My God, that man wrapped in one of my towels was a sight for sore eyes. His chest. Argh! How I never threw myself at him, I'll never know. Oh, yeah, he was bruised, that's why. It's been a couple of weeks since that day. I think it might be safe now for me to propel myself at him without risking injury. It's a nice thought. Just thinking about him makes me...*

'Are you entering the scarecrow fancy dress competition too, Matilda?'

Tilly jumped out of her about-to-get-very-steamy daydream. Her eyes focused on the tall dark-haired woman standing the other side of her stall.

'Oh, no, wait,' added the woman before Tilly could speak. 'You always look like that.'

'Do you want to buy something, Dana?'

Dana's face twisted up with a look of disgust. 'You sell food.'

Tilly was slightly lost. 'Yeah?'

Dana waggled her perfectly manicured fingertips. 'Do I look like I cook?'

You look like the bitch that you are.

'What do you want then?'

Dana's eyes rolled towards Rory, with a look that said she definitely wanted to eat him. 'Hello, who is the new boy?'

Tilly sighed inwardly. 'He's poor.'

'He's hot.'

'He's unavailable.'

Dana looked sharply at her with a snarl normally only seen on an aggravated dog. 'There's no such thing.'

Oh, sod off, you horrible cow. No one likes you, you know. I don't know why you even bother showing your face. It's not as though anyone smiles your way, and Rory certainly won't be smiling at you, or doing anything with you, for that matter, not if I can help it. Go scrape your claws somewhere else. You know, like the underworld, where you were obviously created.

Tilly hated any interaction with Dana Blake. The woman brought with her a waft of stale air, a negative attitude, and left everyone wondering if she had a coat made of 101 Dalmatians hanging up in her wardrobe at home.

'The trouble with you, Matilda, is you have low expectations because, well, look at you.' She tipped her head to one side as she rolled her eyes up and down Tilly's body. 'Don't you think you are a little too old to wear your hair in a plait? You really should do more with your frizz bomb, and I'm not even going to talk about your lack of makeup. Don't you want a man?'

'She's already got one,' said Rory.

Tilly tried to look perfectly natural as his arm swung around her shoulder.

Dana faltered for a moment. 'Oh, hello, you must be...' She waited for him to fill in the gap.

Rory made her wait a few seconds before he introduced himself. 'The name's Rory. Tilly's other half.'

Dana made no attempt to hide what she was thinking. 'Really? That's your type?'

Tilly caught his eye.

Yep, she said that out loud.

Dana wasn't finished. 'You know, whenever she stands still, crows land on her head.' She giggled at her own joke, thinking she was hilarious.

Tilly frowned. 'Erm...'

'Good thing I like crows,' said Rory.

His strong arm pulled Tilly closer, and she responded by putting her arm around his back, so tempted to shove her hand into the back pocket of his jeans and give his lovely bum a quick squeeze.

Oh God, Rory, I really could right now. What would you say if I slowly stroked your bum? Would you like that? Flipping heck, Tills, you need to stop fantasising. It's his fault, being all sexy in my bath towel. Why can't I get that image out of my head? Why didn't I tell him that I thought he looked marvellous and that I wanted to ravish him there and then on the bathroom floor without a care in the world? Because he made me a useless idiot with his toned chest and tight stomach. Wish I had a tight stomach.

'Beauty but no brains, I see,' said Dana loudly, without caring who was listening.

Tilly grimaced inside as Dana winked at Rory.

'Call me if you ever want a real woman, Rory, or maybe just a quickie. I won't tell Worzel Gummidge here.' Dana smirked and walked off.

Rory was clearly gobsmacked for a moment. He gestured down the walkway. 'Is she for real?'

'Oh, you'll get used to Cruella popping up every now and again. Just ignore her. I do.'

'I'll just get back to Jamie. I'm in the middle of a pep talk, trying to get him to talk to the girl who hasn't stopped looking over at him since she arrived.' He lowered his head and kissed her cheek.

Tilly's heart rate accelerated.

Why did he do that? Dana has already left. There's no need to keep up the act.

Part of her wished he had kissed her mouth instead. His busted lip had healed, so there wasn't that excuse. She cast her mind back to the night she had slept in his arms. Not for love nor money could she get the thought out of her head. Every day since, his presence in her bed consumed her mind.

Her mum had moaned about her staying at the shop alone. Her dad had secured the whole building. Bobby had worked in the shop for a couple of days, refusing to leave her alone, and Rory had gone back to sleeping in his cottage.

She felt so lonely every night, even Rex's late-night video calls did little to help. He had taken to calling to read aloud one chapter of his latest book that he was sure she would enjoy. It was pretty decent of him, and Tilly loved reading, but Rex wasn't Rory, and Rory was the only company she craved.

The Sandly Harvest Festival brought joy to her heart, because she fixed it so that she would spend the day working the stall with Rory, and even though they weren't holding hands, hugging, or snogging each other senseless, which she kept daydreaming about, they were close and that was good enough, for now.

Whatever Rory said to Jamie, it worked. Tilly held her breath as she watched her nephew approach Robyn. She quickly exhaled before she passed out, wishing so hard she could hear what was being said.

Robyn blushed, and Tilly hoped that Rory hadn't told Jamie to say anything inappropriate. Jamie had his head held a little higher than normal and a smile on his face that helped reveal just how cute he was. He gestured down the walkway, and Robyn nodded.

Maybe if I just go over there, I can hear what's going on.

Rory grabbed her arm, stopping her from leaving the stall. 'No, you don't. Leave them alone.'

She huffed as she turned to him. 'What? I was just going for a mooch over to the cheese stall.'

He looked totally convinced. 'Sure.'

The top of her brown cardigan was straightened by him whilst intensity filled his eyes, and suddenly Jamie and Robyn had disappeared from her mind. Rory's big hands were close to her face, and she could see him in that towel again.

I wonder if it's rude to ask him how he got those two scars by his waist. I want to see them again. I want to put my hand over them. Touch his naked body. Kiss his naked body all over. I want you, Rory Murphy. I want you right now.

Rory was still staring at her. His hands slowly slid down from her neck to her shoulders. His teeth scraped over his bottom lip whilst he started to twiddle with her dungaree straps.

Tilly waited for him to tug her forward. It seemed like that was what he was thinking. She hoped that was what he was thinking.

Do it, Rory. Scoop me up into your arms and kiss me.

He moved his hands to the edges of her cardigan and wrapped them closer together, then turned away, leaving her standing there dumbfounded and in need of a chair.

What is this man doing to me?

'Rory?' She quickly cleared her throat as he turned.

Good grief, I just sounded desperate.

'You looking forward to the barn dance tonight up at Pepper Pot Farm?'

Oh, great save, Tills, I think.

He tipped a pretend hat and grinned widely. 'Aye, miss. I've been practicing my moves all week. Let's just hope someone wants to dance with me.' He winked, and Tilly wasn't sure if another hot flush was coming on or it was just him.

'I'll dance with you,' she blurted out, unsure but unashamed.

He stepped forward, taking her hand. She twirled into his arms, and he dipped her low. They laughed, and he pulled her up.

The woody scent coming from his tee-shirt caused her heart to flutter. They were so close again, and he had stopped smiling and was staring at her mouth. Tilly held off from swallowing the moisture that had built up in the back of her throat. Oxygen had left her brain, and energy had left her legs.

I'm going to kiss him.

She almost stumbled as he quickly let her go, turned away, and served a customer.

11

Rory

It wasn't quite the country affair that Rory thought it would be. Sure, there was a big barn, twinkling lights, and straw bales, but there were also dressed tables, polished wooden flooring, pop music, and not one piece of gingham in sight.

Everyone was dressed up for the night, but the lack of cowboy hats was disheartening. One of Rory's friends in prison had set up country dancing lessons at one point. He had entertained it for two weeks, just for the craic. He was hoping they would finally be of some use, but nope.

He smiled to himself when he saw Jamie walk in holding Robyn's hand, and he wondered if love was less or more complicated at that age. He glanced over at the makeshift bar in the corner and watched Tilly talking to a man much bigger than him, who was the owner of the farm they were on. He couldn't help thinking the man looked like an American wrestler and wondered if farming had produced his obvious muscles.

Rory casually raised one hand when the big man smiled his way.

There were lots of friendly faces surrounding him, and many of the locals had introduced themselves, welcomed him to the community, and made the robbery at The Post Office Shop the main topic of conversation. Rory got a few pats on the back, he had shaken hands a lot, and many thanks were passed his way. He was quite the centre of attention for the first hour of the party.

He couldn't help but wonder how different his life would be if things at the shop had gone the other way. Tuck pinning Tilly on the freezer still flashed though his mind every so often, causing fury and regret to burn through him. He hated that night. Well, parts of it.

Sleeping on his own each night, worrying if Tilly was settled in her bed, had started to make him a bit anxious. He wasn't an anxious man. Never had been. Little bothered him, and the fight with Tuck sure as hell didn't leave any lasting impact. He could fight anyone and not feel any way about the issue at hand. He would close down, get stuck in, and come out on top or bottom. What had happened to Tilly was different. The thought of her getting hurt brought alive feelings inside of him that he didn't know existed.

She was smiling and chatting happily at the bar, a drink in one hand, the other flapping around as she spoke. She seemed fine, unscarred by the event that took place, but he was still worried. She was only human, after all, and so was he.

When he woke with her in his arms, all he wanted to do was make love to her, but he knew that wasn't on the cards. She'd had a shock, and his body was aching. He wasn't as young as he used to be and knew that healing would take a bit longer. He'd enjoyed her shower, her shampoo, the scent of her in the room, and in particular, the intense way she had looked at him when she saw him standing there wrapped in her towel.

There was something tugging at Rory, telling him to walk away. Leave the farm behind. Leave her. He didn't want to. Life felt good with her in it. He smiled more when she was around, and he longed to see her throughout his day. Still, the feeling was there. He always listened to his gut, but this time he wasn't exactly sure if it were his instincts talking. Whatever it was, he didn't appreciate its input.

A wide smile spread across his face as Tilly approached.

'Hey, you, how you doing?' she asked, touching his hand.

A lot better now you're with me.

A slow song was playing, and a few couples were dancing over by the back of the barn.

'Dance with me, Tilly love.'

She nodded and placed her drink down on the nearest table and took his hand.

Rory looked down at the soft features staring back at him. The twinkling lights glistened on her dark hair, and those big chocolate eyes were smiling his way.

My God, Tilly Sheridan, you really are something.

Their eyes were locked as they slow-danced on the wooden flooring. He lowered his head so that his face was close to hers, and she pressed her head onto his.

His breath caught in his throat as her cheek rolled against his tense jaw. Her mouth was so close to his, he felt it was right to move away slightly. His mouth rested on her shoulder until she snuggled further into his chest.

Every part of him wanted to just take her straight home to bed.

Could I really go there? What would change if I kissed her? What would happen when my time here is up? I'm not going to mess her about. I don't want to hurt her. I don't want to hurt myself.

He pulled her back to look at her and instantly saw the affection in her eyes.

She's falling for you, Rory Murphy. Are you going to let that happen?

'I'm going to get a drink, Tilly.' He left her arms and made his way to the bar, not daring to look back.

Grabbing a small bottle of orange juice from a tub filled with ice, he headed outside.

The sun had long gone to bed, and the air was no longer warm, but it was still a mild enough night, even so, Rory was pleased he had a long-sleeve shirt on. He went over to a large stack of hay bales and sat down, facing away from the noisy barn. He swigged his juice and glanced up at the starry sky.

Can you see my life, Mum? See how I've turned things around? I just hope you have something to be proud of now. Brag to the other angels about how well your boy is doing. I am doing well. A bit confused at the moment, but doing okay. What would you say to me, I wonder? What would I say to you? I'd be interested to know if my old man is up there with you, that's for sure. I'm not sure if he was always a big eejit, or you dying drove him to drink. I kind of get the feeling that losing the woman you love can take you to a place worse than hell itself. Have you seen the girl I've been talking to? Tilly Sheridan. She's nice. Kind. You'd like her, I'm sure.

'Mind if I join you?' said a male voice.

Rory looked over to see a dark-haired man holding the same bottle of juice as him. 'Pull up a pew, my friend.'

The man sat by his side and smiled. 'I'm Josh Reynolds. We haven't met yet, but I've heard all about you.'

Rory was humble. 'Ah, I'm done talking about that, Josh.'

Josh chuckled. 'I bet. This is such a small place, where everyone knows your business. There's no escape.'

'Yeah, I'm starting to notice.' Rory glanced at the juice Josh was holding. 'You not on the hard stuff either?'

Josh shook his head. 'I'm an addict, so that's a no-go zone for me. Alcohol never did me any good.'

Rory thought about all the fights he had got into whilst drunk. 'Me neither.' He gestured back at the barn. 'Bit noisy for you in there?'

'Yeah. I'm not really into parties anymore. That was my way of life once, so I kind of enjoy the peace now.'

'You seem so young to say that. What are you, early-thirties perhaps?'

Josh nodded. 'Yeah, but I spent many years burning the candle at both ends. I'm done with that life. I'm having a baby now, well, my wife is. It's early days, but I'm ready to be a family man. You got kids?'

'No. Never wanted any, not really.'

'I spent most of my life not knowing what I wanted. Well, except for one thing. My wife, Joey. She grew up here on this farm. I met her when we were kids. My gran grew up here too, the top end of Pepper Lane, a place called Starlight Cottage. She used to bring me here for the summer every year, and Christmas sometimes. Joey and I just gravitated towards each other.'

'I met a Joey. Tall, blonde, pretty woman, works in a place called Edith's Tearoom, down the bottom end of Pepper Lane.'

'Yeah, that's my Joey.'

'She told me to pop in her shop for a free slice of cake as a welcome-to-the-bay gift.'

'Yeah, she's like that. One of the many things I love about her. I've loved her since we were teenagers. She was the only person who could make me breathe again when life was shit, you know?'

Rory breathed out a laugh through his nose. His thoughts turned to Tilly. 'Yeah, I know.'

Josh glanced over his shoulder and gestured back towards the barn. 'I'm pretty close with my brother, but it's different with Joey. It's hard to explain. Took us long enough to get together. Long story, but basically, I'm an idiot for not telling her how I really felt about her. You shouldn't leave stuff like that. You just waste time.'

Rory started to wonder if Josh had been sent to him to teach him a lesson about love. He believed people met for a reason. He glanced up at the stars once again, grinned, and then raised his bottle. 'Here's to the women who drive us insane, and may the men of this world one day use their fecking brain.'

Josh laughed as he chinked bottles.

Rory took a swig of juice. 'My old dad used to say that.'

12

Tilly

Bobby shuffled around some papers on the pine kitchen table. 'So, I'm working the till, Mum's at the shop, and you, Tilly, will be running the hot drinks kiosk.'

'Is Dad going to dress up as a pumpkin again this year?'

Bobby grinned. 'Yeah. It does wonders for our business. We get tagged left, right, and centre with pictures of him with families.'

'I think he enjoys it more than them.'

'Yep.'

Jamie scuffed his chair back, standing to get a glass of water from the tap. 'I'm in the field this year, helping with wheelbarrows, if anyone struggles.'

Tilly cupped her hands together in front of her chest. 'Oh, I love our little Pumpkin Sunday. It's so much fun.'

'Yeah, when it doesn't rain,' scoffed Jamie.

Bobby glanced at the window. 'It's supposed to be nice. We're having a mild time of it this autumn, although some nights are cold. Have you noticed?'

'Hmm. I told Rory to help out wherever he's needed on the day,' said Tilly. 'He was surprised we didn't sell our pumpkins at the Sandly Harvest Festival.'

'Did you tell him that we used to?' Bobby shook his head as he turned to Jamie. 'People just didn't want them that early. Our one-day event two weeks before Halloween always works best. We sell out every year doing it that way.'

Jamie placed his glass down on the table. 'Yeah, well, as long as no one expects me to dress as a pumpkin, I don't care.'

Bobby wrinkled his nose at him. 'It's Halloween in a couple of weeks. You will want to dress up then, no doubt.'

Jamie grimaced. 'I'm not five. Anyway, there's talk about going up to the Inn on the Right for a party.'

Both Tilly and Bobby gasped. Her frown lines were hard as she glared at her nephew. 'You can't go up there and party.'

Jamie nodded. 'Why not? Frank died. He won't care. Plus, you've seen the state of the place. That hotel is perfect for a Halloween party.'

A wagging finger came his way from a tutting Bobby. 'It's breaking and entering. You can get arrested for that.'

'Don't exaggerate.' Jamie huffed and sat down. 'It's just a few kids hanging out at a haunted hotel for a few hours.'

'No, it's not,' snapped Tilly. 'Frank's only been gone five minutes. He'll have family that own that place now. Besides, the Renshaws are in the hotel right next door. They'll come over and kick you out.'

Jamie laughed. 'Yeah, right. Like they'd care.'

'You're not going, Jamie,' said Bobby. 'It's trespassing, and who knows what else.'

'And you're certainly not taking Robyn over there either.' Tilly cast him a significant look.

Jamie grinned and offered his palms. 'Fine. I won't go. No need to make a fuss.' He took his water and left the kitchen.

Tilly and Bobby locked eyes.

'He's totally going to that party,' said Bobby.

'Not if I can help it.'

Tilly left the farmhouse and took a slow walk over to Rory's. She figured he might be the one to talk sense into Jamie, or at least tell him what being in a cell feels like.

The smile that hit Rory's face when he opened the door filled her heart with warmth.

Oh, flipping heck, Rory Murphy, why do you have to be so gorgeous? Do you even know how amazing your smile is? How do you not have a queue of women at your door? Obviously, not this door.

'And what brings you here this late, Tilly love?'

'I want to talk to you about Jamie.'

His doorway widened. 'You'd better come in then.'

She kicked off her boots, smiled at the burning fire, and snuggled down into the sofa.

'Make yourself at home,' he mumbled with a chuckle.

He joined her side, and she quickly moved closer to him and flopped on his chest. She couldn't help herself. It was becoming a habit. His chest. Her head. They seemed a good match.

Smiling as his arm came around her, she closed her eyes for a few seconds and just absorbed the moment, unable to process the sensation taking over.

'What's wrong, Tilly?' His voice was soft, husky, and reaching into parts of her that she thought had buggered off with approaching menopause.

Oh, he feels so good. I don't think I can keep my composure much longer. I don't want to. Right. That's it. I've had enough of this.

She raised her head and kissed him.

At first, he just froze, and Tilly wasn't sure what to do with her mouth, but then his lips moved. Slow and steady at first, almost teasing her, and then their kiss deepened. His mouth was warm, and she could feel the heat rising in her.

In them both. It seemed to last forever. But that wasn't something that bothered her. The amount of clothes between them was the thing annoying her the most. She wanted him. All of him.

Rory pulled back, a look of amused confusion filled his face. 'I thought you wanted to talk about Jamie?'

'I did. I do. I just…' She grabbed the back of his neck and pulled him to her mouth.

Rory made it clear he wasn't interested in having a conversation either.

Their bodies slid down the sofa, with Tilly heading towards the rug. Rory's arms held her in mid-fall as their heated kiss intensified. He gently lowered her to the floor and then followed. Her arms quickly fumbled with his top, and he helped her remove it swiftly.

She took a breath, staring at his chest. The swirls of salt-and-pepper hair. The solid muscle created to help ease his mind. His heavy but controlled breathing. She swallowed hard, then went back towards him for more, tugging at his jeans with one hand and getting tangled with her dungarees with the other.

Rory twiddled with her strap. 'It's stuck.'

Continuing to kiss him, she managed to keep one eye on her clothing and free herself from its hold. He quickly swiped off her top, both of them refusing to unlock lips as they undressed, one item at a time.

'Oh God, Rory,' she moaned, and he pulled her closer into his naked body.

They rolled over on the rug, closer to the fireplace. Lust consuming them. Her hand trailed across the greying hairs on his chest, loving the softness between her fingers. His mouth took her neck, and she arched her back for him in response as his beard tickled her skin. Their mouths met again as their bodies frantically tried to become one.

'Ow!' Tilly yelped.

Rory quickly lifted himself. 'What? What did I do?' He looked just as flustered as she felt.

'You didn't do anything. It just hurt down in my lady garden.'

He widened his eyes. 'Your what? What did you call it?'

She blinked slowly as she stared up at him. 'Lady garden. I think it's a nice interpretation.'

There was an obvious smirk being held back on his face. 'Interpretation? Erm… Aye, well, okay.'

She tried not to laugh and pulled him back down towards her. 'Come back here and kiss me.'

He didn't need asking twice. Their mouths locked, their hands reached into each other's hair, and their bodies once more tried to connect.

'Ow!' she yelped again.

Rory shot up. 'Tilly, what's wrong?'

'I don't know. It just really hurts every time you try to…' She pushed him back and sat up, looking down at his manhood as though she was about to dissect the thing.

Rory glanced down to where she had just grabbed and let out a low moan. 'What are you doing?'

'I was just examining it.'

'Yeah, I can see that, but do you know how long it's been since I had a woman's hand down there?' He took a breath. 'If you're going to hold it, Tilly, you need to… Wait, what exactly are you examining me for?'

'I wanted to see if you were super-big.'

'Super-big?'

96

'Yeah, like enlarged or something, and maybe that's why it's hurting.' She frowned at his groin. 'Looks pretty average though.'

Rory raised his brow and corners of his mouth. 'Seen many, have you?'

She ignored the question and moved onto all fours. 'I think we should try a different position. See if that works.' She glanced over her shoulder, wondering what the hold-up was. 'Rory, do you want to try?'

There was a faraway look in his eyes. 'Hmm? Yep, I'm with you.'

'Ooh, wait. My knees hurt. They're not as strong as they used to be.' She lowered to the rug. 'Try now. You'll have to hold me up a bit.'

The heat from his body entered her back. 'Are you sure you're comfy now?'

She giggled at the smile in his voice. 'Yes.'

His lips were on her shoulder, and Tilly moaned out his name. She watched his fingers grip the rug and really wished she was facing him so that she could wrap her arms around his body and sink her fingertips into his bare back.

'Ow!' she yelped.

Rory sat up.

Tilly glanced over her shoulder. 'Lie behind me. Try that.'

He nodded and slowly lowered himself to her side. His mouth was on her shoulder again, then trailed up her neck.

'Oh, Rory, I need you to make love to me.'

'I'm trying, Tilly love.'

'Ow!' She jolted upright. 'Ow, bloody ow! I'm getting the hump now. What should we try next?'

Rory sat up and laughed. 'I'm sorry. I'm not laughing at you. Honest. It's just, I feel like we doing the Kama Sutra here.'

Tilly breathed out a laugh and flopped her head into her hands. 'Oh God, it's so not funny, it's funny.' She raised her head when his hands came to rest on hers. 'Oh, Rory, what's wrong with me? It never used to hurt. I feel broken.'

'Hey,' he lowered her hands, kissed her knuckles, and pulled her closer. 'You're not broken, you hear.'

'Well, something's not right. Maybe it's because I haven't had sex in six years.'

'Six years? I thought your man passed away four years back.'

It felt strange hearing Rory call Lucas her man. She felt that Rory was her man, and now she didn't know how to feel.

'He did, but we hadn't had sex for two years before he died.'

Rory's face was blank. 'Oh.' He pulled in his lips, giving the impression he was holding back from saying anything else about that subject.

'How long has it been for you?'

He gave a half-shrug. 'I was locked up for fifteen years, and I haven't been out five minutes.'

She flopped her head on his shoulder. 'Oh, Rory, I'm so sorry.'

He lifted her face. 'What are you sorry about?'

'That I'm… you know. I can't…'

'Hey, you have nothing to apologise for. I have a beautiful naked woman sitting on my lap right now. I'm as happy as a pig in mud.' He kissed her, which only caused her to try to make love to him one last time.

'Nope.' Disappointment filled her soul. 'It's not happening.'

'What do you want to do?'

'I'm thinking a trip to see the doctor would be the next step.'

He nodded his agreement. 'You want me to go with you?'

'No, I'll be fine, but thanks. It's probably nothing to worry about.'

He arched an eyebrow, kissed her cheek, and looked deeply into her deflated eyes. 'And meanwhile.'

'Meanwhile what?'

He carefully placed her backwards onto the rug and kissed her mouth and then her neck, and then he lowered himself to her stomach. He rolled his eyes up, and she caught the twinkle in his gaze.

'What are you planning, Rory Murphy?'

His grin widened. 'There are more ways to plant a flower.'

Tilly burst into an eruption of giggles. 'What does that even mean?'

He shook his head. 'I don't know. I'm being daft. Your lady garden has rendered me an eejit.' He kissed her belly button and then lowered his mouth to the inside of her thigh.

Tilly continued to laugh, then stopped when a wave of desire hit her body.

13

Rory

Pumpkin Sunday was cold, but a good crowd still turned up to pick their own pumpkins for Halloween. Rory was helping out anywhere he was needed, mostly spending time on the field with a wheelbarrow, removing the rotten or broken pumpkins that weren't going to sell.

He was having a good day and couldn't stop smiling. Tilly pretty much occupied his mind, and every time he passed by the hot drinks kiosk he caught her eye and winked.

He couldn't get enough of her and was eagerly waiting for her doctor's appointment so she could find out why sex was so painful for her, as he was longing to make love to her in every way. He prayed it wasn't anything serious. The thought of her being ill played on his mind. It was too much to bear.

Rory had never felt like a lucky person. His life didn't exactly hit all the marks along the journey, but he had tried so hard to turn his life around, and the fact that he had met Tilly when he wasn't expecting to ever be with a woman again was the biggest surprise and bonus he could have ever imagined. For once, everything felt perfect. He still didn't feel good enough for her, but loving his life at Dreamcatcher Farm overruled all negative thoughts.

He laughed, watching Joseph, dressed as a pumpkin, having his picture taken with a bunch of kids. Jamie was taking even more pictures of pretty much everything, ready for the farm's social networking sites. Robyn was almost hanging off his arm, and Rory wondered if he should have a birds-and-bees chat with the lad. He already planned to talk to Jamie about breaking into a hotel.

It wouldn't hurt to casually slip it into the conversation somehow. I'll ask Tilly about it first. It's not really my place to teach the boy about safe sex. I've got to get out of mentoring mode. I'm not inside now. I don't do that work anymore.

A tall man in a hurry accidentally nudged Rory's arm as he passed him by, waking him out of his thoughts. Rory went to say something but the man was already off the field. He could see the man looked flustered about something. There was also a slight limp he had in one leg, so Rory wondered if the man had hurt himself on the farm.

What's his problem? Maybe I should go see.

Someone tapped Rory on the back, gaining his attention. 'Excuse me, can I get your help, please?'

He turned to see a woman around his age and less than half his height. 'Sure, miss. What would you like help with?'

She gestured her hand towards two large pumpkins close by. 'I was wondering if you wouldn't mind helping me take these two back to my hotel.'

He raised his brow slightly and smiled. 'Erm, hotel?'

She pointed behind him. 'I'm staying at the Inn on the Left. Do you know the place? It's just over the river through there.'

'Aye, I know the place. Just across the little bridge.'

'You see. It's not far, is it? I'm checking-out tonight and only came over here to see what this day was all about. I'm a travel writer, and this is a good local event that I'll be adding to my blog.'

'Oh, well, be sure to let everyone know that Pumpkin Sunday happens every year on the Sunday that is two weeks before Halloween.'

She nodded and revealed a thin-lipped smile. 'That's the plan. Anyway, now that I'm here, I figured I can't go home later without a couple of pumpkins for my twin boys. They'd go spare if they found out I was at a place like this and didn't buy any.'

Rory blew out a laugh. 'Oh, I see your dilemma there.'

'My car's back at the inn, and it's such a short walk, but I can't carry those two big lumps. I'm stronger than I look, and normally I'd give it a good go, but I had a knee operation recently, and, well, I'm not supposed to put any strain on my body. Would it be a terrible bother for you?'

'No bother.'

'Are you sure?'

He picked up the two she had chosen, one practically resting upon each hip, and gestured with his head for her to start walking. 'Lead the way, miss. You can pay me when I drop these off for you at your hotel.'

She smiled as he stepped to her side. 'I'll tip you as well, of course, when we get back.'

He beamed her his best smile. 'No bother.'

'Oh, no. I have to give you something for your trouble. It's only right.'

They headed through some trees, and Rory wobbled slightly over some fallen branches. 'You give this farm a good write-up. That's payment enough.'

'I'll be telling my followers how friendly everyone is in Pepper Bay.'

'Aye, it's a friendly place all right.'

'I'm Justine, by the way.'

'Rory.'

They stopped at the tram tracks and looked both ways.

Justine checked a few more times. 'I know you can see quite clearly if the tram is coming along, but these tracks still make me wary.'

Rory laughed. 'I know what you mean. You think if you place one toe on it, something will come whizzing out of nowhere and take you to your maker.'

She nodded in agreement. 'Exactly.'

'Come on, it's empty.'

They crossed quickly and headed into some evergreen trees.

Justine smiled widely and sighed. 'It's lovely being surrounded by greenery, don't you think? I live in a city, so not much open space.'

Rory thought about his prison cell. It had taken him a while to get used to being confined in such a small space. He never realised how much he had taken for granted before being locked away. The first night was by far the worst. He didn't cry, like some, but he wanted to. A part of him really wanted to. He just found it hard to cry or allow his emotions to appear. It wasn't anything he did on purpose. He was just closed down on the inside. There were times when he wondered if he had a normal heart like other people, because it sure as hell didn't feel like he had.

'I do love the open space,' he said quietly, talking mainly to himself.

Approaching a small, arched, wooden bridge, Justine waggled her finger at the river. 'Ooh, what's that?'

It took Rory all of two seconds to realise that the thing bobbing in the water that Justine had noticed was a child. He dropped the two pumpkins and ran as fast as he could into Pepper River.

A little girl was crying and flapping her arms, doing so well to stay afloat in the current that was pulling her along the middle of the waterway. Her head dipped below the surface every so often, but somehow she was managing to swim back up.

Rory grabbed her whilst Justine called 999, screaming down the phone for an ambulance, a coastguard, river rescue, or whatever they used for a potential waterway drowning.

The little girl spat water as Rory grabbed her hand. He pulled her into his arms and swung her onto his back. 'Hold on tight.'

She did as she was instructed and, with little to no swimming experience, he got her safely to the bank.

He gasped out the cold that was burning his lungs from the freezing temperature of the water. 'Quickly, go back to the farm. Get help.'

Justine ran through the trees, and he turned to the shivering child. 'You all right, little miss?'

She was shaking badly and looked pale. 'I want my daddy.'

'Okay, let's go find him and get you warm.' He pulled away the weeds wrapped around her legs and stood, scooping her up into his arms. He quickly carried her towards Dreamcatcher Farm, rubbing her back to help with circulation.

Christ, I can't believe I just jumped in a river. Ah, this poor kid, she must be scared half to death. What a thing to happen to you. She seems to be holding up well enough. Kids are resilient. She should bounce back quickly. Oh, who am I trying to fool? I've still got plenty of psychological scars from my childhood. Trauma is trauma, at the end of the day. I just hope she's not too traumatised by this that it affects her life.

'He's going to be mad,' she said, her tiny teeth chattering.

'Who, your daddy? Oh, no, he won't. He'll be pleased you're safe. Now, tell me, little miss, what's your name?'

Her blue lips trembled. 'Kasey.'

'Pleased to meet you, Kasey. My name's Rory, and how old might you be? I'm thinking sixteen.'

She giggled, making him feel better that she had perked up. 'No, silly, I'm five, but I'm going to be six soon, and I'm having a mermaid birthday party. That's why I was looking in the river. Do you think mermaids swim in the river?'

'No, I think they stay in the sea, but I do happen to know that they like children to stay away from the water if they don't have a grown-up with them, because it can be dangerous.'

'I'm a good swimmer.'

'Aye, that you are. I saw you.'

'I don't like swimming anymore.'

'You can't let that scare you away from swimming now, Kasey. What you have to do is learn from your mistake. That will help you grow, so it will. Just remember what you did wrong, and don't do that again.'

She snuggled further into his chest. 'I'm cold, Rory.'

'Aye, little miss, I know, but you'll be warm soon. I promise.'

It seemed like the whole of Dreamcatcher Farm ran at him as he stepped out onto the dirt track of Walk Walk Road.

The tall man who had nudged him earlier in the field grabbed Kasey from his arms and held her tightly.

You must be Dad.

A blanket came out of nowhere and was flung around the little girl as fuss and chaos quietened a touch. Joseph started to move the gathered people away, encouraging Kasey's dad to follow him up to the farmhouse.

105

Large arms threw themselves around Rory. 'Thank you for saving my niece.'

Rory went to speak, but the man who had a similar look to Kasey's dad walked away with Joseph.

Another set of arms wrapped around him. This time it was Tilly. She peppered kisses all over his wet face.

'Bloody hell, Rory Murphy, you'll be the death of me.' She tugged him through the lingering crowd, towards his house.

The hot shower on his body felt good, and seeing Tilly's big smile waiting for him when he got out was even better.

She shook her head in astonishment. 'Are you all right?'

Everything feels a little bit surreal at the moment. I still can't believe it happened at all.

'Aye, I'm fine. Any news on the little girl?'

'The paramedics are up at the house now. She's shaken up but okay. She's a good swimmer that kid. Takes after her dad. He could have gone pro, you know, but never did. I guess he taught his kid to swim before she could even walk, which isn't a bad idea. We all need to know how to survive in water.'

'That probably helped her, but there were weeds tangled around her feet. I'm thinking maybe that was pulling her under. I don't know. I'm no river expert. I can just about swim.'

She came closer, making it her business to help dry him with the towel. He grinned down at her fussing over him and decided to let her get on with the job. She leaned up and kissed him hard, taking his breath away for a second.

'You're a brave man, Rory.'

He wasn't having that label. After everything rotten he had done in his life, he did not feel he had the right to be called anything good. 'I did what anyone would do.'

'You just said you can barely swim, and yet, you still jumped in the river.'

'There was a nipper drowning. I didn't have time to think about swimming abilities.'

'Come on, get dressed. We'll go up to the house and see Kasey before she goes home. I think her family will want to thank you.'

'I'd rather not.'

'They only live across the river, and Kasey's dad comes in the shop all the time, so you'll have to face them at some point. Might as well get the thanks out of the way now. Then, you and me can go back to mine and settle down for the evening.'

'As nice as that sounds, there is still loads of work to do out there. The day isn't over, and people want their pumpkins. Oh crap, Justine.'

'Who's Justine?'

'The lady I was helping when we came across Kasey in the water. I was supposed to take her pumpkins back to her hotel.'

'Oh, I saw Jamie helping her as we were heading back here. I'm sure she'll be fine. You were going above and beyond with that customer.'

He raised his brow and grinned widely. 'Is that a touch of the green-eyed monster you have about you there, Tilly love?'

She slapped him with the towel.

He laughed and kissed her. 'It pays to be nice, you know. She's a travel writer and will be mentioning this place in her next blog, I'll have you know.'

'Well, that's all right then.'

He laughed again. 'Oh, so you don't mind me having an affair if it gets you a five-star review?'

'I might as well get something out of you cheating on me.'

He grabbed her arm as she went to get some clean clothes for him. His voice was low and filled with warmth. 'Hey, just so you know, I would never cheat on you. You're the best friend I've ever had. There's no one else I'd rather spend time with. You make me believe in magic, because that's how life feels whenever you're around.'

Tilly smiled. 'Did you get that from a book?'

'I actually just made it up, and I thought I did a grand job of it too.'

She kissed his lips and mumbled, 'You did.'

'I think it's safe to say that I might have fallen for you a tiny bit, Tilly Sheridan.'

Her dark eyes rolled his way, warming his heart and stirring the butterflies in his stomach. 'I might have fallen for you too, Rory Murphy. You know, just a bit.'

14

Tilly

'It's Halloween in a few days. Have you had that chat with Jamie yet?' Tilly looked up from the fish pie she had just placed in her oven.

Rory shook his head in disbelief. 'I haven't seen you all day and that's the first thing you want to talk about? I want to know how you got on when you saw the doctor.'

Oh, yeah, that. I was trying to avoid this chat. Not exactly the best topic of conversation nor one I thought I'd be having with anyone. Oh well, here goes.

She slumped down onto a kitchen chair and huffed. 'I saw the doctor. I don't have a problem. I'm just perimenopausal, that's all.'

He sat at her side, none the wiser. 'What does that mean exactly?'

'It means me and estrogen are getting a divorce, and it's leaving me behind with a whole heap of crap to deal with by myself.' She glanced down as his hand covered hers.

'Hey, whatever is happening in your life, just know you are not by yourself.'

Tilly slumped her neck further into her shoulders, and his hand gave hers a gentle squeeze. 'I bought some lubricant to help with the dry matter, and I've been given some estrogen cream to try.' She gestured towards her lap.

'Dryness? That's the problem?'

'Aye,' she huffed out.

Rory laughed at her Irish accent. He leaned forward and swiped her hair away from her cheek. 'Well, now, that's not so bad.'

He's kidding, right?

Her eyes shot up so fast, they could have rolled right out of her head. 'Not bad? Not bad? Of course it's bad. If I want to have sex, I have to whip out a tube of lube just as the moment gets heated. Talk about mood kill.'

Did I just say tube of lube?

His face was flushed with amusement. 'What are you talking about, woman? People stop in the moment for something all the time. Condoms, for one. Handcuffs maybe, or whatever tools they're into.'

'Tools?'

'Yeah, gadgets and whatnots. I don't know. All I know is, it's not a big deal to use a lubricant in the grand scheme of things.'

She took a deep breath and lowered her head as though the weight of the world was on her shoulders. 'Feels like a big deal, Rory.' She smiled as his hand stroked her cheek.

'Tilly love, you want to try it now, see if it works?' His voice was so warm and husky and filled with a smile, she couldn't help but laugh.

'Well, the fish pie will take a while to cook, so we have some time.'

He grinned widely. 'It's such a turn on when you talk to me like that.'

She stood, slapping his elbow. 'Come on then.' She attempted a seductive walk to the bedroom but tripped over her own foot and stumbled into the doorframe. She quickly regrouped and beamed a big smile his way.

Rory kissed her hard as soon as he stepped inside the bedroom, causing her knees to weaken and her heart to race.

'Oh God, Rory, this better work.'

He smiled against her lips. 'Don't worry, I have a backup plan.'

She smiled back, fizzing with electricity. 'I like your backup plan.'

'I know you do.'

Within seconds, their clothes were on the floor, their naked bodies on the bed, and their embrace locked almost as close as they could go.

His warm touch was melting her everywhere, and his strong kiss was taking her almost over the edge. Her hand shot out to the paper bag on the bedside cabinet, rummaging around with her fingertips, frantically trying to remove the lubricant and condoms she had bought after her trip to see the doctor.

Rory stopped kissing her and looked over at what she was doing. He pulled the bag to the bed and removed the items. He arched an eyebrow along with the corners of his mouth. 'Strawberry gel? What are we supposed to do with this? Eat it?'

Tilly grimaced, remembering her time spent looking at the shelves in the shop, feeling completely lost. 'There were so many in the chemist. I didn't know which one to try. I thought this might smell nice.'

He laughed. 'Aye, well, there's that.'

'I bought condoms too.'

'I can see that.' He eyed the two large boxes by her side. 'Do you think you bought enough?'

'It was buy one get one half price.'

He kissed her nose and grinned. 'Sounds like a good deal.'

She pulled the tube out of its box as Rory went back to kissing her neck. Just for a moment she forgot what she was holding, as her body started to melt into his again.

Their need for each other was at an all-time high, and she let the tube slip from her fingers so that she could cling on to his back. She wrapped her legs tighter around him and gasped when he let out a low moan.

'Ah, Tilly, hurry and open the bloody thing.'

She fumbled around on the bed for the tube, found it, and held it between their faces. 'Wait, I haven't read the instructions.'

'What instructions? We just put it on.'

'On you or me?'

'I don't know. Both?'

'How much do we use?'

Rory leaned up onto his elbow. 'We're going to use the lot.'

'Then we might not feel anything at all.'

He grinned down at her. 'I don't mean in one go. I just mean in one night.'

She laughed and opened the cap. 'Oh, wait, there's a seal.' She peeled it off, not realising she was gripping the tube so tightly. A small blob of strawberry lubricant spat out of the tip, hitting Rory straight in the right eye.

'Ow!' He clasped his hand to his face.

'Oh my goodness!'

He sat up quickly, holding his eye. 'Ah Jesus, Tilly. It bloody stings.'

She tugged him out of bed. 'Quick. The bathroom. We need to rinse it out.' She practically pushed him all the way there and up against the sink.

Cold water was splashed on his face before he even had time to remove his hand from his eye. It hit his chest, making him shudder.

She quickly draped a towel over his back. 'Is it coming out?'

'It's like I've got glue in my eye.'

She faffed around him as he continued to wash over the sink. 'It smells nice.'

An eruption of laughter filled the bathroom.

'I'll give you smells nice, Tilly Sheridan.'

She leaned over his back and softly kissed his neck whilst giggling. 'I'm sorry, Rory.'

He turned to her, one hand clasped over his eye, and smiled.

'How is it now?' she asked quietly, trying to hold back her laughter.

He removed his hand to reveal a bloodshot, slightly swollen eye. 'You look blurry.'

She chuckled. 'Probably an improvement.'

'There's nothing to improve, except maybe your aim.'

'I wasn't aiming for you.'

He turned back to the sink. 'Hmm, lucky shot.'

Tilly laughed again as she headed for the door. 'Let me quickly check on dinner. I'll be right back.'

Great! I can't believe I did that. Oh, don't laugh. Of all the places it could have landed, it had to be in his eye. I don't know whether to laugh or cry. Oh my goodness, it was funny. I have to stop grinning every time I look at him. And I really need to stop running with no bra on. I'm going to knock myself out with a boob in a minute.

The pie was cooking nicely, so she turned on the heat for the vegetables to boil, then made her way back to the bathroom.

Rory had removed the towel from his back and was dabbing his sore eye. 'You ready to put that gel where it's supposed to go?'

She grinned widely and propelled herself towards him. He scooped her up into his arms, and she wrapped her legs around him, causing him to stumble back a step. Her mouth pressed down hard on his, and he tried to carry her out of the bathroom with only one working eye peering over at the door.

Tilly couldn't stop kissing him and didn't want to either. Everything about the man turned her on, even his temporary squint.

They laughed as he manoeuvred them out of the room, bumping her knee on the doorframe, his elbow on the bedroom door, and also when he tripped on their clothes strewn over the floor.

Finally, they were back in bed.

'So, here we are again.' He attempted a wink, but failed miserably with only one functioning eye.

'Just you, me, and the strawberry gel.'

'I'm never going to look at strawberries the same way ever again.'

She chuckled and got busy with a condom and the gel. Her dark eyes smiled his way as she wiped her gooey finger down his cheek. He shook his head as he grinned, and she kissed his other cheek and whispered, 'When you're ready, Rory love.'

His laugh was muffled. 'Yes, miss.'

She went to say something else, but a feeling she hadn't felt for so many years washed over her, leaving her momentarily speechless. Her breath caught in the back of her throat, and she could tell by the change in his breathing and the affectionate way he was looking at her that he was feeling the same way.

Just for a moment, there were no words to be spoken, no sounds to be made, and no movement.

Bubbling water spilling over on the oven from the boiling veg caused them both to wake from their brief trance.

'Are you going to get that?' His words were breathy and seemed to be a struggle to say.

'I don't think I'm ever going to move again.'

The corners of his mouth twitched. 'Do you mind if I move?'

She frowned with disappointment. 'Where are you going?'

'Oh, I'm going nowhere, Tilly love. I'm just going to move right here.'

Their smiling mouths met, and Tilly closed her eyes and fell even more in love.

15

Rory

The sea was calm under a blue sky that stretched out from Pepper Bay. Rory sat on a small wall and stared at the gentle rolling waves that foamed up upon the shoreline. The salty air and cry of a seagull made him smile from the inside out. It wasn't often throughout his life he had seen the sea, but whenever he did, it made something within him feel calm.

It was quiet down at the small shingle beach. No one was paddling or walking their dog. No one was behind him by the shops in Pepper Lane, and no one was by his side, keeping him company.

The sound of the water was soothing, and the mildness of the day helped relax him. He still wore a coat, but it was flapped open, revealing a thin blue jumper that was suitable for the end of October.

I could do with sunglasses. It's bright today, and my God, it's beautiful. There really are some amazing places on this planet. I wish I could see them all. I don't ever want to go back to London again, and I sure as hell don't want to go to Cork. Not much to welcome me there. Could I even be trusted to go back to London? Yeah, sure I could. I think. No, I could. I'm different now. I wouldn't slip back into my old ways. I just wouldn't. I know many who do. That's a scary thought. I'll stay away. I don't suppose there are many from my old circle floating about nowadays anyway. I know half of them are still doing time, and some are dead. Maybe some got out of that way of life. Changed their life too. Lots of folk change their life. I hope some people I know did. I want us all to succeed. Am I a success? I don't know.

He closed his eyes and absorbed his surroundings, taking a few deep breaths and finding his peace. It was only when he met Nik that he started his journey towards inner peace. So much turmoil filled his life. He was pleasantly surprised when he discovered a way to relax that didn't involve alcohol.

Had someone told him years ago that he would one day be sitting on a wall on the Isle of Wight, meditating in front of the sea, he would have laughed in their face.

Each slow, deep breath was as soothing as sunbathing on a summer's day, and Rory wished every moment of his life had felt that way.

He would see the other kids out and about, having fun with their parents, going on holidays and days out. Hear them talk about what they had for dinner, and watch as they crowded around the ice-cream van with their money pointing up at the rocket lolly picture on the side. He wasn't sure how old he was the day he stopped wishing and dreaming to be someone else. To be somewhere else. He simply just merged into the life he had been given and accepted the damn right ugliness that came with it, knowing he had no choice. There was no point wanting to be the kid at the park playing footie with his dad, and there sure as hell was no point wishing he had someone at home cooking him a hot meal and fixing his torn clothes.

He opened his eyes.

I have to let the past go. All of it, not just London. I can't change anything. I can't grieve for my childhood. My life is happening now, and I have to keep my head in the game. Be present, Nik says. Aye, but the bloody past likes to make itself known every so often. I can't live there. I live here now.

117

Everything is different here. I have myself a girlfriend, I think. A wonderful woman with a heart of gold. I still don't know how something so good landed on my lap, but I'm grateful for her. Something will go wrong eventually, so I'm grateful for now. I'll appreciate the time I do have with her. I feel I'm being negative about this, but I've always been poxed. How am I supposed to feel about this situation I'm currently in? How am I expected to just know what to do when the going gets good? I should talk to Nik about this. He always has a great point of view that makes sense.

'Hey, Rory, you look relaxed down there.'

Rory turned to see Josh approaching him. 'Hello, Josh. You all right, mate?'

Josh joined him on the wall and glanced over at the sea. He turned his collar up and smiled. 'It's mild but you still need your coat, don't you?'

'I bet it's lovely down here in the summer.'

'Yeah, and over in Sandly. I don't know if you've seen it yet, but there's a long stretch of golden sand over there and loads of colourful beach huts.'

Rory straight away imagined himself walking along the beach, holding hands with Tilly. 'What's not to love about a beach.'

'I never used to be someone who stopped to smell the flowers, so to speak, unless I wanted to draw something, but now I just take in all my surroundings, and I'm grateful for it all too.'

'You a bit of a spiritual man, Josh?'

He nodded. 'I am now. I met this man called Rusty. He's like this guru type, and he changed my life. Well, he helped me change mine.'

Rory thought of Nik. 'I have a fella in my life like that. God bless them.'

'I read a lot now too. Spiritual stuff. Thought-provoking books, that kind of thing. I'm seeing who I relate to, who makes sense to me, and who doesn't. It all helps. Dead or alive, some people's words are helpful with my growth. Others, not so much. But you have to broaden your horizons, as they say, to see what's a fit for you out there. Do you read much?'

Rory's mind went straight to the prison library. 'Not as much as I should. Maybe I should take a look at some of your books, Josh. See what works for me.'

Josh nodded. 'Sure. I also do video meetings sometimes, if you ever want to join in. Rusty's in New York. He's Scottish, not American, but he has a foundation out there, so he's there most of the time. We have group chats about stuff like gratefulness, and we practice breathing techniques. It's like a mindful class, of sorts. You're welcome to join in.'

'That actually sounds like my cup of tea, but, unfortunately, I don't have a laptop or even a phone.'

Josh was clearly trying to hide his confused surprise by that statement, and Rory felt comfortable enough with him to explain a few things.

I think you, Josh Reynolds, are someone who would understand me. My life taught me not to be trusting, but my gut tells me you're all right.

'I've just come out of prison, Josh.' He could see he had the man's full attention. 'Fifteen stretch. My mentor got me the job up at Dreamcatcher. He helped change my life while I was still inside, about ten years ago now. So I know all about change. I'm a big fan of psychology. And all the crap that happened in my life has somehow made me more of a spiritual kind of person, a bit like yourself, I guess. All I know is, I think differently now. I react differently, and I like myself. I'm so far away from the man I was, you know?'

Josh nodded. His bright azure-blue eyes softened as he turned. 'I know, mate. I'm disconnected from the old me too. Sometimes I can't believe he existed. Do you mind if I ask what you went inside for?'

You wouldn't be human if you didn't want to know. No one wants to sit with someone evil.

'Robbery.'

'Oh.'

'Back in London. So, you see, when I came here to rebuild, I didn't have any money, and I earn little now. The job I have up at the farm is just to help me find my feet and give me something decent to put on my CV for when I want to move on.'

'That's good of the Sheridans to do something like that to help you. I'm going to have to mention that to my brother. See if we can introduce something like that in our company. There's help out there for young offenders, but perhaps we could offer something for older offenders who have changed their ways, like you. We could call it something like… The Rory Project. I don't know. There's a man who works for us who is good at all that. He'll know the best roads to go down. We probably won't take on all ex-crims though. You know, it will depend on the crime.'

'That makes sense, and it is pretty decent of you to want to be involved too. Not too sure about The Rory Project, though.' He chuckled and Josh joined in. 'You'll have to talk to Nik down at Shine. He can work with your man.'

'Yeah, we'll set that up. Someone once helped me turn things around, so I feel as though I'm now paying it forward. I'd like to do something like that.'

Rory gave him a gentle pat on the back. 'You're a good man, Josh Reynolds. So, what does your company do?'

'I'm one of the owners of Café Diths.'

120

Rory almost choked on air. 'Bloody hell, they're everywhere. You own that? Wow! Didn't know I was sitting with such a businessman.'

Josh grinned widely, revealing perfect teeth. 'I'm no businessman, that's for sure. I'm an artist. That's what I prefer to do. My brother runs the company. He lives up the top of Pepper Lane in Starlight Cottage, with his wife and new baby, but we have a team over in London who keep the cogs turning.'

'I would say you're probably the richest man I've ever met, but we once had this posh bloke banged up with us for a while. Not sure what he was doing with his taxes, but the Sheriff of Nottingham wasn't happy, that's for sure. The man was a funny lad. Spoke nice, like yourself, but didn't even know how to make his bed, so that was a bit of a novelty for the rest of us.'

'I'm glad I never ended up in prison. Ended up in a few gutters though.'

Rory chuckled. 'Ah, similar thing, Josh mate.'

'I actually woke up once with my face in a muddy puddle. I'm surprised I didn't drown. You can, you know. I still don't know how I got there. A lot of my past is a blur.'

'I got punched in the face once in a pub by some bloke who said it was his revenge for me breaking his fingers. To this day, I have no idea who that man was. My friend confirmed I had done that to the poor fella, but I was blind drunk at the time. That's why I didn't remember him.'

The two men sighed as they both turned back to face the gentle lapping of the waves upon the shore.

'It can be a funny old life, eh, Rory?'

'Aye, Josh, it can.'

Josh's face perked up. 'Hey, I've got a spare laptop back home and a phone you can have, if you want. Then you can join in with our meetings. Rusty would love to have someone like you on board, especially for the newcomers who need people to look up to. You've got a great backstory. The kids will definitely listen to your experiences. What do you think?'

'You want to give me a laptop and a phone? Just like that?'

Josh gave a half-shrug. 'I have lots of old phones just sitting around. Joey's always moaning at me when I buy a new one. Reckons I waste money, which I probably do, but I'm just used to buying the latest. Sorry, I sound like a spoiled rich kid. Not going to lie, I am one, but still.'

They both laughed.

'You might as well take them, Rory. The laptop doesn't get used. It was wiped clean a while back, so all ready to go. I can show you how to use it, if you don't know how.'

Rory nodded. 'Oh, I do. We had computer lessons inside. I know the basics. Are you sure about this? I'm not used to people giving me things.'

Josh placed one hand on his shoulder. 'Yeah, come on. I only live up there at Honeybee Cottage. We can grab them on your way back home.'

'That's pretty decent of you, Josh. Thanks.'

'No worries. Now, have you tasted my wife's cakes yet?'

Rory followed Josh's eyes over to the quaint pale-pink shop called Edith's Tearoom. 'Not yet.'

Josh stood and nudged him. 'Come on. Let me introduce you to the bay properly. Oh, and don't worry, your past is your past. I won't tell anyone your business. That's totally up to you, mate.'

The wonderful aroma of fresh coffee filled the air as Rory stepped inside the tea shop. He glanced around at the pink gingham tablecloths and then at the floral bunting draped across the two windows either side of the door. His eyes then rolled over to an array of sweet goods sitting in a counter towards the back of the shop, and then he saw the internal door that led upstairs to the flat above the shop and then the doorway for the kitchen at the back.

He couldn't help how his eyes wandered around anywhere new that he entered. It was programmed in him to inspect a place on entry, and he still hadn't managed to stop himself from checking out escape routes, potential earners, and security. He sighed inwardly at his old habit, then focused on the muffled noise at the back of the shop to help distract himself.

Josh's wife, Joey, poked her head out of the kitchen door. 'I'm just icing some Halloween biscuits. Oh, hello, Rory. Have you finally come for your free slice of cake?'

He smiled widely and tipped his head towards an old lady sitting by the window as he called back to Joey. 'Aye, miss. If that's okay.'

'You can sit with me,' said the old lady, bringing his attention back to her.

Josh gestured towards her with one hand. 'This is Joey's gran, Josephine Walker.'

'Hello, Josephine, and how might you be?'

'All the better for seeing you, Rory Murphy. I've heard loads about you already, but I already knew things about you before they all did.'

He raised his brow in amusement. 'Is that so?'

'Sit down,' called out Joey. 'I'll bring some tea and cake over. And, Gran, leave him alone.'

Josephine's wrinkly brow lowered, causing a squint in her beady eyes. She grumbled something under her breath as Rory and Josh joined her table.

'Josephine knows everything,' said Josh, grinning as though someone had just whispered a joke in his ear.

Rory had met plenty of old folk like Josephine before. He had little doubt she did know things that most didn't. He could see her eyeing his hand that was resting on the pink gingham tablecloth. He flipped it over and offered his palm, which she gladly took.

'You see that, Josh,' she croaked. 'He's not afraid.' Her eyes rolled up for a second to meet with Rory's. 'They're all afraid when I look.' She went back to reading his palm and started mumbling to herself.

Josh shook his head at him. 'You're a better man than most, Rory.'

'Ah, it's not my first reading.'

'Your only accurate one though,' said Josephine.

He leaned into her. 'How much is this going to cost me, Josephine Walker?'

The corner of her mouth almost twitched into a smile. She ignored the question and remained concentrating on the reading. 'You've had some past, Rory Murphy.' She kissed her middle finger and gently pressed it into his palm.

What was that? Was that kindness? Some sort of kiss on the hand? She's a strange one, but I like her. She reminds me of my great-aunt Ciara. She was always reading the tea leaves and turning the cards. So, Josephine, what have you got for me then?

'Not sure I want to give you any spoilers,' she said, as though reading his mind as well as his palm.

'Aw, go on now. Give me something to help me sleep at night.'

Josh rolled his eyes, and Josephine smiled.

'I'll give you something, son. When the times comes, choose home. That's the place where you belong.'

Home? Home as in London, or home back in Cork? Either way, I don't want to go there. I don't want to belong there. Thanks for that message, Josephine. That will definitely help me sleep at night. Great!

16

Tilly

It was late, and Tilly was alone indoors with only her old photo album for company in bed. She stroked over a picture of Lucas sitting beneath a tree one summer after a feast of a picnic and a kiss under the sun. That was a good day. They were so in love and had kissed and snuggled close for most of the day, not wanting to be apart. He had told her about his dream to work with a new organisation that helped ex-offenders rebuild their life. He was so excited to be part of something that would bring more positivity to the world, as he hated anything negative.

A tear fell down onto the plastic sheet covering the photo, and Tilly quickly wiped it away. She turned the page and smiled at the photograph of her and Lucas dressed up for a night out. There was a charity ball at a restaurant in Sandly called Swan Lake that was raising money for the local donkey sanctuary, and she remembered how glamourous everyone was, and how suave Lucas had looked in his tuxedo. They were in their early thirties then, not that either of them looked their age.

Her bleary eyes gazed across the room to stare at a painting on the wall of some ducks waddling towards a river. Rory was in her mind and guilt was in her heart.

I'm so sorry, Lucas. I never meant for this to happen. I didn't know I would meet him and feel the way I do. I didn't expect to ever feel this way again. Not ever. I miss you. I really do, but he's in my heart, and it feels so natural.

She closed the album and placed it under her bed and picked up a hardback notebook and a pen that had a duck stuck to its top.

The pages were filled with letters to her little sister. Something she had been doing for years. If she needed someone to talk to, or had something exciting to report, it would go in one of her notebooks. Tilly called them her letters to heaven. She pulled a pillow over to her lap and placed the notebook on top. Chewing on the duck-pen, she pondered over where to start.

Dear Luna. You're not going to believe what's been happening to me lately. Firstly, Dad hires a new farmhand. Bobby and Rex think he has a touch of Paul Newman about him, but I just see Rory. That's his name. Rory Patrick Murphy. Needless to say, he's Irish. Well, technically, he's English, as he was born in London. That's what he told me. He has a lovely soft accent and a kind demeanour about him. I warmed to him straight away, and I feel as though I've known him forever. It's a bit strange. I think you'd like him. The family seems to. Mum invites him for dinner a lot, and you know she doesn't do that often. Jamie's really taken to him, so I'm hoping Jamie listens when Rory tells him not to go to the Halloween party over at the Inn on the Right.

I'm torn, Lulu. I think I'm falling in love with Rory, but I feel as though I'm cheating on Lucas every time I think about him, and if I'm honest, I don't think about Lucas that often anymore. That sounds so bad, doesn't it?

Rory saved the shop from a robbery. He saved me too and nearly got arrested for his trouble. It's been a crazy couple of months. I'm not sure how long he is going to stick around for. I'm a bit scared to have a proper conversation about it, if I'm honest.

Oh, yeah, Jamie has a girlfriend. Robyn Sparrow. Actually, I think her last name was changed to Walker. I'm not sure, but she's Tessie's daughter, so you know who I mean. There's been a lot changes in Pepper Bay this year. Tessie and Nate finally got married. Like I didn't see that coming. Joey married Josh, and even Jake Reynolds got married. That, I did not see coming. He has a baby now. Were you watching? Did you see Scott at the birth? Joey's pregnant. Dolly's Haberdashery changed to a gift shop, but you already know all about Dolly. It's been a busy year, and it's not over yet.

I wish I knew how it would end for me, Lulu. I wish I could just enjoy my time with Rory without having these guilty moments. I know Lucas would want me to be happy. He was a good man.

Love you, Luna Butterfly.
Miss you every day.

Tilly's phone bleeped with an incoming video call from Rex. She put down the pen to answer.

'Hey, Rex. You're calling late tonight.'

'I know, honey, I'm sorry, but Bobby was extra-worrying about you tonight, so I wanted to check you were okay.'

'Extra-worrying? Well, yeah, that sounds like him. I'm okay. I was just writing to Luna.'

'Oh, well, that tells me you're not okay at all, Tills.'

She sighed quietly away from the screen. 'I've been looking at photos of Lucas tonight.'

'You feeling guilty?'

'Yep. Is it that obvious?'

Rex smiled warmly and flapped one hand in front of his chin. 'It's natural, but you know what Lucas would say about this situation, and you know he would like Rory too. That big hunk of a guy has been nothing but sweet to you, honey. You know he has.'

'I know, Rex, and I really like him, but...'

'No buts, Tilly Sheridan. Life is too short. You have been given a second chance at love. That's something to smile about not cry about. Don't add complications where there aren't any. You two met, you fell in love, you're having a great time, except for the robbery, of course, but, you know, life for you is good right now. Don't you go ruining it by overthinking.'

'It doesn't sound complicated when you say it, but I can't help it if Lucas pops into my head every so often and messes with my feelings.'

'Honey, Lucas will always pop into your head from time to time. You were together for years. He was a huge part of your life, but your life has changed now, and it's time for you to accept that.'

Tilly smiled at him smiling at her. 'I've slept with him.'

Rex's smile widened as far as it could go. 'Ooh, details.'

She snorted out a laugh. 'I'm not giving you details. Just, it went well.'

Rex raised his brow in astonishment. 'It went well? What kind of statement is that? It went well. What was it, your first driving lesson? Come on, Tills. Went well?'

'We had some problems at first. That's what I meant. In the end, it was... wonderful.'

'Oh, you mean he couldn't... perform?' Rex held his mouth open and a sympathetic look in his eyes whilst one finger swirled around, pointing down at his lap.

'No, not that. It was me. I ended up having to buy a lubricant.'

Rex scoffed. 'Oh, honey, that's not a big deal. I buy that.'

Tilly raised a hand. 'I do not want to know about your sex life with my brother, thank you very much.'

Rex chuckled. 'I'm just glad it worked for you. Did you buy a plain one or…'

'Strawberry.'

He nodded as he pursed his lips. 'Pineapple is my favourite.'

'Can you really get so many different ones?'

'Oh, Tills, you'd be surprised by the things you can buy for sex. I know a guy who wears full-on rubber suits that he has custom-made, and his partner wears one too, and they make it work.'

Tilly was dumbfounded. 'How does it work if they're covered in rubber?'

'I asked that too. Apparently, the suits have secret pockets, of such. You can guess where.'

She didn't want to guess where. She didn't want the visualisation. 'I guess lubricant is quite a mild aid in the grand scheme of things.'

Rex clapped his hands in front of his monitor. 'Ooh, you could try roleplay. Perhaps be a prison guard.'

An eruption of laughter filled the bedroom. 'I hardly think that will turn him on, Rex. More like make him plot an escape.'

'Yes, you could be right there.'

'Anyway, I happen to think we don't need anything else. It was perfect the way it was. So natural, you know. I feel as though I've known him for ages.'

'That's a good thing. It was like that when I met Bobby. We just clicked straight away. God, I love that man.' He started to flap one hand in front of his face, fanning himself. 'Oh great, now I'm going to cry.'

'Don't cry, Rex. Why don't you do something different this year, and come for Christmas?'

He sniffed and straightened up. 'You know what, Tills. I just might.'

'We could make it a surprise.'

He clasped his hands over his chest and let out a small puff of air. 'I love that idea. I'm totally doing it. I'll book my flight so that I arrive on Christmas Eve. Oh, Bobby is going to cry. I'm so excited already. Oh, wait, I'm supposed to be cheering you up.'

Tilly laughed. 'I'm okay, Rex. Honest. I think I'm going to pop over and see Rory right now.'

'It was all that talk of rubber suits that got you going, Tills.' He laughed.

'No. I don't want that image in my head. Each to their own. I won't judge, but I don't want anyone else's sex life in my head, thank you.'

Rex waved her away. 'Oh, go on then. Go be with your man. And Tilly… don't make trouble where there isn't any. Enjoy your life, honey. Okay?'

'Okay.'

'Love you, sweetie. Bye.'

'Bye, Rex. Love you too.'

As soon as she hung up, she jumped out of bed, shrugged on her dressing gown, put on her wellies, and headed downstairs.

The air outside was cold and fresh, and the sky was clear, revealing a thousand stars twinkling high above her. The sight warmed her body, and the thought of snuggling up to Rory warmed her heart.

I'm coming, Rory love. You can bet on that, and you're going to be more excited than Bob when Rex turns up on Christmas Eve. Oh, Christmas is going to be so good this year. I hope Rory is still here. I'm going to ask him to be. I'm going to talk to him about his wants and wishes. I need to find out if we're on the same page. I need to know how much of me he wants. Flipping heck, I feel a bit nervous now.

She plodded down the dirt track, skipping over the cracks, knowing all the dips to avoid. She stopped at his door and took a breath.

I'm not usually this worried. Maybe I could save the chat for another time. Perhaps we can just snuggle tonight. Oh crap! I forgot the strawberry gel. I'll have to buy some for his place too. What a thing to have to think about every time I go out now. Keys, phone, money, lube.

She muffled her laugh with her hand, then knocked on the door.

Rory's smile was wide, beaming, and sexy as hell, and Tilly practically fell into his big arms.

Their mouths locked as she tugged at the back of his neck, running her fingers up into his hairline.

He picked her up and managed to close the door with one hand.

Tilly was peppering kisses all over his face. 'I missed you, Rory. I...' She stopped when she noticed an opened laptop and what looked like a brand-new mobile phone sitting on the table. Clambering down from his body, she gestured with her head towards the gadgets.

Please, no. Tell me he didn't steal those.

She glanced at him, then back at the items. It was obvious he could read her mind, as his face fell as flat as hers.

'Where did you get those from?' The words were out of her mouth before she had time to think about what she could say. There was no denying the fact that she was accusing him of stealing. It was written all over her face and in the sharp tone that came out in a hurry.

Rory's body language didn't give away any clues, but his eyes had lost all softness. 'You think I stole them, don't you?'

She faltered, not knowing what to add. If he had slipped back into his old ways, there was no way she could forgive him. There was no way she could have a future with a thief.

'Did you?' she asked sharply, unable to lose the fury that was building inside.

'Is that what you think of me?'

There was definitely an injured tone to his voice, and the one second flash of sadness she caught in his eyes made her feel like instant crap.

'You say that like you're not a thief.'

Oh no, why did I say that? Take it back, quickly.

'Was a thief, Tilly. There's a difference, but I wouldn't expect your kind to understand. You've just proven that.'

'My kind?'

'All high and mighty. Little Miss Girl Guide. I bet you've never so much as taken a penny sweet.'

'No, I haven't. Why would I? It's not about the worth, you know. If it's not yours, you've no right to it. You want a penny sweet, go out an earn some money so that you can buy one.'

And I know that's a valid point.

'I think you should leave now, Tilly.'

'That's fine with me, because I don't want to stay anyway.' She glanced over at the laptop and phone.

'Yeah, I stole them. Go call the police on me. Go on.'

133

The childish way he produced his statement left her speechless for a couple of seconds. She swallowed hard, trying desperately to roll back the tears that entered her eyes. Rory's body softened. He took a step closer. 'Tilly, I...'

She held out her hand, stopping him in his tracks. 'No.'

He huffed loudly. 'I didn't steal the bloody things, okay, but thanks for the vote of confidence. I really appreciate it.'

She wanted to leave but needed answers. Sniffing back her emotions, she asked, 'Where did they come from?'

'Josh Reynolds gave them to me. You can call him and check.'

'I'll do that.'

He clenched his teeth and shook his head in disbelief. 'Aye, I'm sure you will. So, can you go now? I want an early night. I have work to do first thing, and your judge and jury presence is keeping me awake.' He walked towards the front door and opened it widely. 'If you wouldn't mind.'

Tilly slowly stepped outside, unsure what else to do. She turned on the doorstep to say something, but he slammed the door in her face.

17

Rory

The Inn on the Right was the complete opposite to the one next door. There were cracked windows, chipped steps leading up to the door, missing roof tiles, and rubbish strewn across the driveway. The whole building was in desperate need of love and attention, and Rory could clearly see why the local kids referred to the hotel as haunted.

What the hell happened to this place?

His eyes rolled over the premises, then towards the shiny, clean, well-looked-after hotel on the other side of a tall dividing fence.

Muffled laughter could be heard coming from inside the derelict building, and flashing torchlights flittered across window panes every so often.

Rory's gut told him that Jamie was inside, and when an empty bottle of cider was thrown out of the opened doorway and landed at his feet, he figured Jamie was probably drinking too.

Well, I guess my chat with him went in one ear and out the other.

He really thought he had got through to the lad as well. They had chatted for ages, and Rory had explained how much trouble Jamie would be in if he was caught breaking and entering. Jamie had nodded, paid attention, and agreed, but Rory knew the lad was young and thinking himself a lot smarter than he actually was. Rory knew how to play the game. Nod, agree, and then go and do it your own way.

He nudged the cider bottle with the tip of his boot and glanced over at the doorway.

It was Halloween night, so it was most likely just a bunch of giggling kids inside and not a crim on a job. The place didn't look as though it had anything worth stealing anyway, and that was just from the outside.

It didn't look much better inside.

Jesus, it smells like someone died in here and the corpse is still hanging around. Go into the light, my friend. You do not want to stay in this stuffy old place. Look at the state of it in here. This is supposed to be a hotel? A working hotel until recently? It couldn't have been. Someone's got their dates muddled. It doesn't look as though it has seen a guest in years. Unless folk stay here for that haunted experience. I don't know what the owner was thinking. It can be a haunted house without being dirty. My God, how thick is that dust? Is it any wonder kids would come here for Halloween.

He walked over to the reception desk and eyed the small selection of chocolate bars that had been dumped there. He picked up a Mars Bar, unwrapped it, and bit off a large chunk.

Might as well.

There were doors everywhere and a staircase leading upwards. He walked towards the broken banisters and glanced up. A roar of laughter caused him to notice a stairway leading downstairs behind an opened doorway.

A huge kitchen that looked as though it hadn't served any food in years was occupied by a group of teenagers drinking cider, giggling loudly, and throwing prawn cocktail crisps at each other.

Rory watched them, unnoticed, for a moment.

I'm guessing mid-teens, the lot of them, and what do you know, there's Jamie, and he looks a tad the worse for wear.

136

Clearly, someone's had one cider too many. Robyn's with him. She looks okay. A little fed up, but with a normal colour about her face, which is more than can be said for young Jamie there. Not sure what shade that is. Vomit-green? Oh, he's going to feel the sting pretty soon, if he hasn't already.

Rory dramatically cleared his throat, but the noisy group didn't hear him.

I could pretend to be a ghost and scare the crap out of them. Ha! Now there's a thought. Jamie would probably faint, by the look of him. Nah, better not. Let's get their attention though.

'Oi!'

The laughter ended abruptly and all eyes turned to the big man standing at the bottom of the stairs. One lad looked as though he had just seen an actual ghost and went as white as the Scream mask on top of his head. Another boy feebly tried to hide behind the tallest girl in the kitchen, who was less than impressed about his cold hands touching her bare arms. Robyn looked ready to cry, two more looked ready to run, and Jamie was about half a minute away from throwing up.

'I think everyone needs to go home.'

No one moved. All still frozen with fright, except for Jamie, whose eyes were almost on the floor, they were that drooped.

'Now,' Rory ordered loudly, making them all jump out of their trance with him.

The group quickly headed for the door, swallowing hard and avoiding eye contact as they passed Rory by.

He held Jamie's arm. 'Not you.'

Robyn was wide-eyed and visibly nervous.

'You stay with us, Robyn. We'll get him home first, then you after.'

Tears were sitting in her eyes, and Rory shook his head as he turned back to the stairs. 'Come on, Jamie. Let's get you home, lad.'

Jamie groaned as soon as his foot hit the first step. 'Ooh, wait. I don't want to move. Don't make me move.'

You're lucky I'm not Auntie Jean. She'd have you up those stairs so fast, you wouldn't know where you were at, and your spinning head would still be trying to find its way out of the kitchen. Her boyfriend would have given you a pat on the back though, and another bottle of cider, no doubt about that.

'You can't stay here, Jamie lad.' He tugged him further up the stairs, with a quiet Robyn traipsing behind.

The foyer was empty. The other kids had cleared out, leaving their rubbish everywhere and their visit long behind them.

Rory balanced the boy against the dust-covered reception desk and turned to Robyn. 'I want you to call your mother, then hand me the phone.'

Reluctantly, she went to do as she was told but stopped as two policemen walked in with one of the owners of the hotel next door.

Rory recognised Officer Brian from the shop robbery. It was obvious the policeman recognised him too, as he raised his brow in disbelief.

'You again.'

Oh, this just gets better and better. What are you going to do this time? Blame me again, no doubt. Accuse me of breaking the lock because I've got form, I know. I bet you went straight back to the station and checked me out.

Authority and Rory Murphy mixed as well as custard and mustard. Ever since he was a child, he was taught that the law was nothing more than a thorn in the side. He wasn't raised to have any level of respect for the police, or teachers, or any adults who weren't family. He had grown up that way. Thinking the worst of the boys in blue. Having no trust in what was viewed as *the other side.*

'They're not here to help the likes of us, son,' Jean would say.

Her boyfriend would join in with a whole heap of swear words to add to the subject, all of them aimed only at the justice system.

Nik had helped Rory with his trust issues, his lack of care for the community, and to grow his respect for those in charge. It didn't come naturally, and it was one hell of a fight at first, but over time, Rory started to see people as simply people, no matter their job. However, it had been many years since he'd had any sort of run-in with the law, and this was the second time since his release. Some of the old vibes resurfaced. He could see himself being profiled in the officer's stern eyes, and there was something embedded deep within Rory that was suddenly knocking on his door, telling him to leg it.

Ignoring his old habits, Rory gestured towards Jamie, who looked ready to pass out any minute. 'We're just leaving. I'm taking these kids home.'

Brian stared around Rory's shoulder. 'What's wrong with him?'

It was quite obvious what was wrong.

'Ah, you know,' said Rory, lightly waving a hand. 'Too many treats, not enough tricks. I blame the old girls. They have a tendency to hand out chocolate liqueurs from last Christmas. Not the best idea, but never mind. He'll be right as rain in the morning, so he will.'

The owner of next door's hotel, Ned Renshaw, burst out laughing. 'Chocolate liqueurs. More like apple bobbing in a bucket of cider.' He turned to Brian and placed one hand gently on his back. 'Come on, Bri. Give the kid a break. We all know how he's going to be punished.' He nodded at Robyn. 'Do you need me to take you home?'

She shook her head and took a step closer to Rory. 'We're taking Jamie home first. I want to make sure he's all right, then Rory's calling my mum.'

Brian pointed over at the main door. 'Who broke in?'

Jamie groaned, clutching his stomach whilst attempting to sit on the dusty parquet flooring.

'I think the lock has been broken for ages,' said Ned, sounding one hundred percent convincing, except to Rory.

Brian turned to him with a face like thunder. 'You never told me that when you called me over.'

Ned shrugged and swiped back his floppy dark hair. His aquamarine eyes flashed over at Rory, and a slight grin tugged at the corner of his mouth. 'Hey, I just heard a commotion and figured it was kids ghost hunting. You know how it is on Halloween, Bri. But you can't be too careful. Anyway, no harm done in the end.'

Brian glanced around and screwed his face up at the state of the place. 'I cannot believe old Frank let this place get this way.' He shook his head, revealing a one-second moment of sadness in his eyes. 'Shame.' He snapped out of the emotion. 'Still, these kids were trespassing.' He glared at Rory. 'Or was it you who came here first?'

Here we go.

'I was just passing, sir. I heard a noise and came inside to investigate.'

Brian wasn't buying that. 'Is that right?'

'Aye.'

'And what exactly are you doing around here at this time of night?'

'I don't know what the time is, but I was bringing over some chocolate for young Kasey's trick or treat bag.' He glanced at the sweets on the desk and smiled.

'Oh, thanks,' said Ned.

Rory picked up a packet of chocolate buttons and tossed it to him. 'Here you go.'

Ned caught the sweets and looked over at a rather unimpressed policeman. 'Rory was the one who saved Kasey from drowning in the river.'

Brian's indifferent expression stayed put. 'Of course he was.' If laser beams could have shot out of his eyes, they would have definitely zapped Rory at that point. 'You're just everywhere, aren't you, Mr Murphy?'

'Good thing he is,' said Ned, before Rory had a chance to speak. 'Rory, come over tomorrow night for dinner at the hotel. We still haven't thanked you properly. No arguments. Six sharp. We'll be expecting you.'

There's no getting out of that one, I guess. It's just a free feed. I can manage that.

He nodded his RSVP.

Brian sighed loudly for all to hear. 'Okay, get the kids home. I'll put in a report that this place needs a lock.' He turned to Ned. 'Do you know who the new owner is yet?'

He shook his head. 'No. Sorry. I can't help with that. Hopefully, they'll let us buy the place or knock the eyesore down. It doesn't help us having this next door.'

Rory bent and scooped Jamie up under his arm. 'Come on, lad.'

Jamie groaned all the way to the door, his feet dragging behind him. Rory contemplated carrying him, but had little desire to end up covered in vomit. He knew drunk people were prone to throwing up, especially when manhandled or bumped about.

Getting Jamie back to Walk Walk Road was a mission in itself. He needed to stop every two minutes, could barely walk when he continued, and gave it his best effort to tell his company that he was going to die, more than once.

'Will he be all right?' asked Robyn, sheepishly glancing over at Rory, then avoiding eye contact when he looked back.

'Don't you worry about him, Robyn. He'll have a rough night of it, then wake feeling like sh… not feeling his best, but then, as the day goes on, he'll be back to normal, and, hopefully, he'll have learnt a valuable lesson.' He studied her face for a moment before dragging Jamie along a few more inches. 'Did you not have a drink yourself?'

'I'm underage.'

He tried hard not to scoff at the casual way she handed over her answer.

'You're all underage, but it didn't stop the others, by the look of them.'

Robyn suddenly looked about thirty years old as she folded her arms and stared his way. He'd seen that look on plenty of women before, but never on a kid. 'I grew up in the pub in Pepper Lane, The Ugly Duckling. I know all about responsible drinking. My grandfather taught me from a very young age. I have no intention of becoming drunk or a drunk. I want to be a vet when I'm older. Drinking is a mug's game.'

Rory couldn't hold back his laugh to that statement. 'Your grandfather taught you that too?'

She dropped her arms and went back to looking worried. 'Yes, but don't tell him I said that. It pays well for customers to down pints.'

'Aye, it does at that.' He propped Jamie against a tree and held him in place with his knee. 'Now, call your mum and give me the phone.'

Robyn's small shoulders drooped as she did as she was told. 'Hello, Mum. Rory wants to talk to you.' She handed it over.

'Hello, Tessie, is it?' he asked, pretty sure that was Robyn's mum's name. He remembered the small, red-headed woman who lived at Pepper Pot Farm. She was a bubbly, friendly sort and made him feel welcome, telling him that as soon as he got a phone, he could join the Pepper Bay WhatsApp group.

'Yes, what's wrong?' Tessie's voice was as shaky as her daughter's.

'No need to worry. It's just, I've got Robyn and Jamie with me, and we're just heading up to the main house here at Dreamcatcher, and I was wondering if there was someone available to come pick her up. It's dark, and I don't want her walking home. I'm happy to bring her back once I've dealt with young Jamie, if you can't get out at the moment. I just...'

'Jamie was supposed to bring her home an hour ago.' Tessie then started to talk to someone in the background. 'It's Rory. Robyn's with him and Jamie. They're... Wait.' She went back to talking down the phone. 'What do you mean, you're dealing with Jamie? What is to be dealt with? What has he done and does this involve my daughter? Is she in trouble?'

Rory could hear a man's deep voice coming towards the speaker on the phone. Tessie started to have a conversation with him again.

'Erm, hello?' said Rory, trying to gain attention.

'My husband is on his way to pick her up.' She thanked Rory and hung up the call.

He sniffed away the cold night air as he glanced down at the small girl.

'My dad's coming, isn't he?'

He nodded sympathetically. She was about to get told off, that much was obvious. In some ways, he thought that was a good thing. Discipline wouldn't have been a bad thing in his childhood. The only time he got in trouble with his elders was when his step-mum was in a foul mood and took it out on him. There was no naughty step or grounding, just a beating for no reason half the time. No one taught him right from wrong. No one in his family seemed to care about that sort of thing.

Rory scooped up Jamie into his arms like a baby, ignored the groaning and the sick-warnings that were coming his way, and marched off to the farmhouse.

Bobby was in the kitchen when Robyn opened the door fully for Rory to enter. 'Ouch,' he cried, slapping one hand dramatically to his head. 'He is going to feel that in the morning.'

Rory carefully propped Jamie up against the sink. 'I think he's feeling it now.'

Bobby glanced over at his nephew. 'Beer?'

'Cider,' said Rory.

Lillian entered the room and froze for a second. 'Is he drunk?' She didn't wait for an answer. She stomped over to the sink and slapped him on the shoulder. 'You, my boy, will be up at the crack of dawn and out on that field, and we'll see how much you like the taste of booze then.'

Jamie reached over the sink and threw up.

Bobby gagged and turned away. 'Oh my days, that's disgusting.'

A car screeched to a stop on the driveway outside.

'That will be Robyn's dad,' said Rory, looking at the door, not knowing how the next moment would play out.

Nate Walker's large frame filled the doorway. His taupe eyes were almost on fire and his thick lips were tensed as soon as he took one look at the slump at the sink.

Lillian waggled her finger out at him before he could speak. 'You say one word about our Jamie being drunk, Nathanial Walker, and so help me, I'll tell the whole bay about every escapade you got up to in your teens.'

Nate's mouth flapped open and closed like a fish out of water. He turned sharply to his daughter.

'I didn't drink,' she quickly told him.

'I love you, Robyn,' Jamie groaned out from inside the sink.

Robyn's hand touched her chest as her eyes turned dreamy and her mouth gaped.

Bobby held the same look, but Nate rolled his eyes and huffed.

'Get in the truck.' His dad tone was on point, but his neighbourly vibe was slightly off when he turned back to Lillian after Robyn left the house. 'She's fourteen.'

Lillian softened her expression. 'I know, Nate, but she's all right. Rory got them back here safely.'

Rory glanced at the muscle man and was pleased to see Nate give him a slight nod of appreciation.

'Cheers, Rory.'

'No bother,' he said quietly.

I need to get out of this family situation. Why did I involve myself in the first place? This is all Tilly's fault, making me some sort of mentor for the lad. Fat lot of good that did. Look at the state of him.

Jamie heaved up an orchard, which caused Nate to leave.

Bobby closed the door behind him. 'Well, that went well.'

Lillian waved him towards her whilst dabbing Jamie's mouth with the edge of a tea towel. 'Take him up, get his PJs on, and settle him down with a bucket. I'll fetch up some water.' She glanced over her shoulder as Bobby led the poorly boy away. 'As soon as I've bleached my sink,' she added to herself.

'Can I help you, Lillian?' asked Rory, unafraid of the splattered mess lining the white basin.

She turned to him and smiled. 'You go home, son. Put your feet up. You've saved the day once again.' She turned, shaking her head at the sink. 'I don't know what we're going to do when you leave. You've had such an impact on the bay.'

Rory stepped back out into the night and breathed in the cool air.

Not sure I want to leave. Even if Tilly thinks I'm still a thief.

18

Tilly

I can't believe I forgot, but then again, we did arrange this back in August. I'm sure I wrote it down somewhere. Oh, never mind. Luckily, Ant sent the email reminder. He's always been super-efficient. He seemed happy enough to still go ahead with the date. I need to perk up a bit, else what am I going to look like all night. I hope Rory doesn't find out, not that it's any of his business what I do. It's not as though we're together. And that would be thanks to me calling him a thief.

Tilly brought her powerwalk to a sudden halt to catch her breath. She stood in the middle of the small bridge that led over to the Inn on the Left, glancing down into the dark water beneath her.

She had no idea why she didn't bring a coat with her, nor why she thought it would be a good idea to dress as though she were off out on a night on the town. Her tights were making her legs feel itchy, not to mention her stomach, and she wasn't sure if that was because they were about twenty years old. The last time she slipped into the little black number she had on was for someone's funeral a couple of years back. She figured it was an allrounder.

She had exercised that morning, hoping it would knock off a couple of pounds. She had also accessorised and glamorised, and now the only other rise was the annoying dress creeping up towards her thighs, making her wonder if she had grown taller in the last couple of years, or did *dry clean only* really mean just that?

A shiver ran the full length of her spine, and she wondered if it was too late to pop back home and get changed.

Surely, Ant wouldn't mind if I was late. He probably would, knowing him. But he is my friend, so maybe he would be okay with it. Oh, sod it. I'm nearly there now anyway, and it'll be nice and warm inside. I'm just fussing. It's nice to dress up from time to time. I rarely get to look this way. I'm happy with my fake-date look. Plus, it'll be nice to catch up with Ant. I've not seen him since the charity event.

Tilly stepped off the bridge and carried on towards the hotel. Her flat shoes helped with walking in the dark, that and the fact she pretty much knew every hole in the ground along the way. She could have done the journey blindfolded. It was so dark by six in the evening, it was as though she was actually blindfolded in some places, especially by the tram track.

She took another breather and another tug of her tights, pulling them up and the dress down, before heading down the driveway of the hotel.

The warmth hit her straight away, and she made a beeline for the crackling fire in the open fireplace in the foyer. No one was behind the reception desk, and the stairway and part of the first-floor landing that she could see were also empty.

The Inn on the Left wasn't exactly running alive with guests during November, but the locals still used the restaurant during the winter to help support the business. Plus, the hotel had an excellent chef.

Some muffled chatter was coming from the dining room across the way from her, and she figured Ant, being the early bird he had always been, was probably already inside having a drink at the bar.

She checked her made-up face in the large ornate mirror that was above a loveseat.

Not too shabby, Tills. Good thing I look younger not older. Although, what is that? Oh wow, my skin looks really dry. My makeup isn't sitting right like it used to. Great! Now I'm drying up on my face too. If this keeps up, I'll resemble a prune before my next birthday.

She raised her chin to check out her neck.

Maybe if I sleep on my back from now on I can help reduce the lines just below my throat. Why have I got lines at the top of my chest anyway? What's that all about? And why am I just noticing this? It must be this stupid mirror. My mirrors at home don't show this much detail. This is one of those dodgy mirror-on-the-wall jobs that's about to tell me I am so not the fairest of them all.

She stuck two fingers up to the mirror.

I know I'm not the fairest in the land, but at least I've got... What? What rhymes with land? I could say man, but I haven't got one of those. Not anymore. Okay, mirror, you win. I'm officially the crusty old lady with the apple.

She sighed to herself, feeling deflated, and turned to the dining room, checking once more to see if anyone was around before faffing about with her outfit again. It wouldn't be a good look to shove her hand up her dress in front of people, so it was now or suffer. There could have been CCTV in the hotel, but that was an afterthought. She only hoped Elliot Renshaw, the eldest of the two brothers who owned the inn, respectfully deleted the embarrassing problem as soon as he clapped eyes on the footage. He was a good mate, so she was pretty sure the final tug of her tights all the way up to her breasts was in safe hands.

Ant smiled his big friendly smile that had toothpaste advert written all over it. She was so pleased to see that he had turned up in a navy suit, as she was worried she had overdressed for the occasion. It's one thing to dress for a

149

date, and another to dress for a mate. Especially one who is only out for the night with you because he pulled your name out of a hat. All in the name of charity. They were both single and game for a laugh, and the local donkey sanctuary was always in need of funding, and Pepper Bay and Sandly were huge sponsors.

The date would have taken place back in August, but Ant had to work overseas, so they arranged it for the beginning of November when they knew he would be back.

Tilly went straight in for a hug, but Ant was a cheek kisser, so that went well.

Breathing in his oaky scent, her thoughts turned to Rory. It was almost as if he were in the room with her. The cologne was obviously strong enough to cause some sort of drug-induced hallucination, because she could suddenly see Rory standing at the bar.

Those grey-blue eyes that usually held such warmth for her went from surprised to intense, then darkened slightly before boring into her soul with a hit of pure desire, which caused the moisture in her throat to stick to her tonsils like glue.

She quickly turned back to Ant because her eyes needed something else to focus on. Plus, swallowing hard was desperately needed, and there was no way her throat was going to work all the time she had eyes on the gorgeous Irishman propping up the bar.

What the hell is he doing here? Breathe, for crying out loud, Tilly. Just breathe. Oh, he looks so handsome in that blue shirt. It really brings out his eyes. Wait. Why is he dressed up? Good grief, please don't tell me he has a date. Oh, don't cry. What are you doing? Roll it back. Get a grip. Ant's staring at me now. I didn't lose a tear, did I? I haven't smudged my mascara already, have I?

She carefully wiped a finger under her right eye whilst smiling at Ant.

'Shall we sit down?' he asked, gesturing towards a table close to the bar. 'Our table is ready.'

Tilly made sure she had her back to Rory. There was no way she was going to stare at him all night. She glanced around the room to see a young couple with a small child over by the window, two old ladies a couple of tables away from the family, and a local couple from the bay, Scott and Dolly.

Her thoughts turned to her little sister, Luna, who had created a bucket list once she found out she was terminal. One of the things she wanted was to have a wedding day, but she was single, so it was Scott Harper who agreed to marry her. They were good friends and nothing more. He had made Luna's day, and Tilly and her family had always loved him for doing that. She smiled his way, happy to see how settled he was in his relationship with Dolly.

I don't think I'll ever stop being grateful to that man.

Scott smiled back, and Tilly turned her focus to Ant.

'It's lovely to see you again, Tilly. How have you been?' Ant's arm crossed the table to rest upon her wrist for a few seconds.

'Oh, you know, fine as usual. How about you? How's work?'

His hand slipped back to his lap as a huge smile beamed her way. 'It's going really well, and I met someone at a conference back in September. She's so lovely, Tilly. I've been walking around with my head in the clouds ever since our first date.'

Tilly laughed, relaxing into the conversation. 'Oh, Ant, I'm so pleased for you.' Their hands met across the table, where she gave his fingers a gentle squeeze. 'Did you tell her about our charity date tonight?'

He chuckled as he nodded. 'Yeah, she knows.'

'You should have cancelled, Ant. I wouldn't mind. We already donated.'

'Don't be daft. What's the world coming to if two old mates can't share a meal.'

'Well, I wouldn't want her to get upset about it, that's all.'

'No, she's cool.'

Which is more than can be said for Rory.

Ned came out of the kitchen, carrying two plates of hot food and gestured towards a table. Rory sat down, joining him for dinner, and they had to go and sit at a table that was now within eyeshot.

How awkward would it be if I asked Ant if we could swap seats? Pretty awkward, I'm thinking. Okay, just leave it. Ned's keeping him occupied anyway. Look, they're laughing about something. Rory's not looking at me anymore. That's good. I think. Right. Concentrate. Ant and his new girl. Yes, great subject.

'So, Ant, what's she like?'

He adjusted his glasses whilst leaning closer, and Tilly caught Rory glance their way. She casually pushed herself back into her chair and sat up straight.

This is an acceptable table distance while still engaged with my date, and hopefully Rory will see only friendship between me and Ant. Maybe I should go and explain what's going on here. I don't want to hurt him. Oh, why am I overthinking this? Rory and Ned are laughing again. Clearly, he's having a better date than me. Right. Back to Ant. What was he saying? Oh crap, he's waiting for a response.

She nodded slowly whilst letting out a quiet humming noise.

'You agree then?' he asked, eyes wide, seeming happy.

'Very much.'

Ant lowered his dark eyes to his twiddling fingers. 'People will say it's too soon.'

I seriously have no idea what we are talking about here. I'm just going to have to wing it.

'Listen, Ant, we're fifty now. We're far too old to worry what people think of us, and we sure as hell shouldn't be waiting around when we know what we want. Life's too short.'

Well, that did the trick. He's perked right up. And great, he's holding my hand again, and Rory is giving him the death glare. Ned's noticed now. He's whispering to Rory, hopefully telling him that me and Ant went to school together. That might settle him. Nope! Whatever Ned just said clearly didn't work, because now Rory's giving me daggers. Oh, stop looking at me and eat your dinner.

'Is something wrong, Tills?' Ant's voice came in loud and clear, jolting her out of her staring contest with Rory.

She gestured Ant closer. 'The big man talking to Ned is my... Actually, scrap that. I don't know what to call him anymore.'

'Your ex?'

'No. Well, maybe. See, I don't know. We're seeing each other, but I went and messed things up, and now he's not talking to me, so I didn't get a chance to tell him about our fake date, and I'm worried he'll think it's real. I don't want to hurt him, Ant. I really care about him.'

'Hey, why don't we invite him over. You can introduce me, and we'll explain about the charity event we went to in the summer.'

'I'm not sure he's ready to listen to anything I have to say. I can't tell you everything, Ant, but...' A sudden wave of heat filled her face. 'Oh bloody hell, not now.'

'Tilly, what's wrong?'

'I'm perimenopausal, Ant.'

'Hot flush?'

She nodded and started to fan herself with the white napkin, wishing she could rip her tights off her stomach, for starters.

Ant moved from his chair to sit in the one beside her. 'What can I do?'

'I'm burning up, Ant. Help me cool down.'

'Okay, erm.' He grabbed a piece of ice from his glass of straight vodka and held it on her cheek. 'Is that any good?'

'Put it down my top.'

Ant dithered close to the top of her breasts as Tilly grabbed the neckline of her dress and tugged it as low as it would go, which unfortunately for her wasn't very far.

'Oh God, I'm so hot.' No longer caring about panting in his face, she moved closer to his icy fingers and moved them towards her neck.

Ant's hand hovered over the top of her dress and was brought to a sudden halt by large fingers clasping down around his palm. 'Ow!' The lump of ice he was holding slipped out of his grip to land in Tilly's bra.

She didn't mind, but Rory seemed to when Ant glanced down at where it went.

Rory's intense stare made Ant sit back. A cold bottle of water was placed onto Tilly's neck, which released a slow moan from her lips.

All eyes were now on her, even the small child in the restaurant had stopped colouring in his book and was looking over.

'Oh, Rory, pour it down my chest.'

He swallowed hard and cleared his throat as she let out another moan. 'Would you mind getting a glass of ice for the lady?' he asked Ant.

Ant looked relieved to have a job that excused him from the table.

Tilly grabbed Rory's hand and shoved it further down her dress. 'I need to get these tights off.' She moved her hand towards her lap, but he stopped her in her tracks.

'Oh no you don't.'

She looked him straight in the eyes. 'I'm so hot, Rory.'

'Hmm, that you are.'

She quickly stood and practically ran out to the foyer, almost knocking the glass of ice cubes out of Ant's outstretched hand. Rory was right behind her and followed her over to the stairs where she flopped down.

'Is it passing?'

She nodded as she gasped, reaching for the bottle of water in his hand.

His hand was on her brow as she sipped the drink.

'Rory, I'm fed up already with this. I don't know how many more I'm going to have.' She closed her eyes for a moment because his gentle stroking motion of her hair soothed her soul immediately.

'It's okay, Tilly love. It's over now.'

She leaned her head into his solid chest and fought back the tears she could feel building. 'I'm so tired, Rory.' His lips were on top of her head, and something about that touch made her want to go home, get into her PJs, and fall straight asleep.

Ant's voice was close as he asked after her, so she opened her eyes and raised her weary head.

'Hey, how's it going, Tills?' His voice was soft and filled with affection. He squatted down to her eye level and held her hand.

'I'm so sorry, Ant. I've ruined our dinner.'

He smiled warmly. 'Don't be daft, mate. It's not your fault, and we can still eat if you fancy it.'

'I just want to go home.'

'That's okay, Tills. We can do this another time. I'll bring my girlfriend, and we can double date or something.' He glanced at Rory.

'Everything all right?' asked Ned, his eyes only on Tilly. Scott was right behind him, also looking for answers.

'Hot flush,' she told them. 'Put me right off eating.' She glanced over at Scott. 'Go back inside, Scott. I'm okay.'

Scott gave a nod and went back to the dining room.

Ant leaned over Tilly, kissed her cheek, and stood up. He looked down at Rory. 'Look, mate, I don't mean to be funny here, but me and Tilly go way back, and I just want to make sure she gets home safely tonight.' He turned to Tilly before Rory had a chance to respond. 'What do you want to do, Tills? Do you need me to take you home? I can call a cab for us right now if you want.'

She could feel Rory's breathing pattern through their touching bodies. It was slow and steady, and his thumb that had been stroking her back had stopped moving.

'You head home, Ant. I'll see to myself.'

'I'll take her home,' said Rory, without a trace of authority in his tone.

Tilly sheepishly looked up at him. 'You will?'

'Aye, if you want.'

'Okay.'

Ned walked over to Ant. 'Why don't you stay and have a bite to eat with me if these two are heading off.'

Ant nodded. 'Okay. Might as well have something.' He turned to Tilly. 'You reckon you could manage a starters before you go?'

Ned gestured his head towards the dining room. 'Or I can wrap up some food for you to take home, Tilly.'

She really had lost her appetite but appreciated the kindness coming her way. 'I'm good, thanks.'

Ned looked upstairs. 'You can have a lie down in one of the rooms if you need to rest before heading off.'

'I'm okay, but thanks, Ned.' She stood, and Rory quickly joined her, holding her elbow. 'I'll head off now. The walk will do me good.' She moved out of Rory's hold to give Ant and Ned a hug and say goodnight.

The cold air outside made her grateful for her tights strangling her stomach. She only wished the chill had entered the restaurant when it was needed.

'Jeez, it's cold.' Before she could say another word, a big coat was flopped around her shoulders.

'Put your arms inside.'

A faint oaky scent filled her nostrils, creating warmth and happiness. Her whole body smiled at being wrapped up in Rory's coat.

'You'll be cold now.'

He scoffed. 'What, after you with your lustful moans and sexy threads. I think I need cooling off.'

'Do you really think I look sexy?' It was a genuine question, because she wasn't feeling it.

A slight twitch of his mouth caught her eye. 'Not going to lie, I do prefer your dungarees, but, yes, you look absolutely drop-dead gorgeous.'

What was that? Was that my ego hitting the moon?

She tried to hide her smile by lowering her mouth into his coat. 'I wasn't on a date, Rory.'

'I know. Ned explained.'

'Oh.'

'You're a free woman though, Tilly. You can date if you want to.'

'I don't think my date would last five minutes with you around giving him the death glare.'

'I guess I'd rather you didn't date anyone other than me.'

She glanced at the blue fitted shirt that he looked so good in. 'Can I hold your arm?'

He tilted out his elbow. 'You not steady on your feet there?'

'I'm fine. I just want to hold you.'

He breathed out cold air from his mouth. 'Oh, so these are your tactics, are they?'

She giggled and leaned further into his side, not moving away until they stood on the bridge. 'Rory, I'm sorry I thought you were a thief.'

He pulled her around so that she was facing him. 'I was once.'

'Oh, stop that. You know what I mean.'

'It's done now. Let's forget it and move forward.'

'You forgive me?'

He placed his hands either side of her face. 'Hey, I'd forgive you for anything. I was all set to drop to my knees and beg you to take me back right there in the restaurant in front of your man Ant.'

It was clear he meant every word. The look in his eyes was filling her heart and warming her more than his coat.

'I love you, Rory.' Her soft voice filled the silence. Even the cold river was still and peaceful.

'I love you too, Tilly Sheridan.'

Their lips met and what started off as a tender kiss quickly heated to one filled with passion and need.

She grabbed his hand and pulled him off the bridge and into the trees. 'Let's do it up against the tree, Rory.'

He breathed out a laugh. 'Erm, okay, but are you sure? It's freezing out here.'

Pressing her back up against the bark, she tugged him closer. 'I'll warm you up.'

He smiled on her lips. 'Oh, is that right?'

'Oh flipping heck.' She pulled her head back to look at him. 'We can't. I haven't got any magic potion on me.'

Rory's brow lifted along with the corners of his mouth. 'Magic potion. Is that what you're calling it now?'

She shrugged into his chest. 'I thought it sounded nicer than lube.'

'Aye, it does, and magic it is.' He wrapped her up in his arms and kissed the top of her head. 'Let's hurry and get back to yours.'

19

Rory

Rory sat on a stripy deckchair, swirling his boot into the golden sand that made the beach in Sandly. He looked up to the dark night-time sky and smiled, feeling content. Tilly was sitting in a blue deckchair to his right, her hand in his upon his thigh. There was something so tranquil about that simple act of sitting together in silence.

The water was lapping gently at the shore, and some children were having a late-night paddle whilst patiently waiting for the fireworks display to start.

'I've never seen a fireworks display at the beach before,' he told Tilly.

She smiled warmly, giving his hand a light squeeze. 'We have them every year down here for the fifth of November. Then we have our own bonfire party up at ours.'

Rory laughed to himself. 'Yes, I've been building it for two days. That took me back. When I was a kid, me and my mates would try to get our hands on as much wood as possible. We'd want the biggest bonfire out of all the flats round our way. There would be parents yelling at their kids for nicking one of their kitchen chairs and all sorts.'

Tilly raised her brow in amusement. 'Did you ever do that?'

'What! Are you kidding me. If I had taken my aunt's furniture to burn on a bonfire, she would have stuck me on it right next to Guy Fawkes. I've done some stupid things in my time, but messing with Auntie Jean wasn't one of them.'

'She sounds like quite a character.'

Hmm. Well, the less said about my mad family, the better.
'We'd have big gatherings around our bonfire, you know. The whole flats would come out. Old and young. We'd light the bugger and set off random fireworks on the concrete ground and hope we'd had enough fun before the fire brigade turned up to dowse the monster.' He laughed out loud. 'Oh, the fights we would have. And not just with the firefighters. We'd take turns to guard our precious bonfire before it was lit. Other kids from different neighbourhoods would creep over to steal your wood. So you had to be on guard.'

Tilly giggled. 'Wood wars.'

'Aye. I'm not even exaggerating. It was serious stuff. All hell would break loose if someone touched your bonfire. That was a big no-no.' He glanced once more at the inky sky above the sea and smiled at his memories. 'This here seems less chaotic.'

'It's only some of us Pepper Bay lot that enjoy the bonfire up at ours. Dad gets the BBQ out, even if it's raining, and we put some music on and have a good night. We've never had to worry about firefighters or anyone stealing our wood.'

Rory playfully nudged her arm. 'Well, aren't you lot the lucky ones.'

She shuffled in her dipped chair, sitting closer to him. 'You'll have to help put it out at the end of the night. We don't leave it to burn out unattended. Not on a farm.'

'Aye, I know. Your dad told me. That's okay. I always wanted to be a fireman.' Rory sighed with happiness, and Tilly snuggled into his arm.

'Do you really like it here, Rory?'

His eyes scanned the many people on the beach, the dark sky, the gentle water, and the stillness that was there even amongst a crowd.

Tilly reached up and kissed his cheek, smiling as he turned to face her.

'I do, Tilly love. I like it here.'

'You fit right in,' she whispered.

Rory breathed out a laugh. 'I'm sure.'

'Hey, you do. I'm glad you're here. I don't think you should be anywhere else.'

He kissed the tip of her nose and gave her a cheeky wink. 'I don't want to be anywhere else.'

'Good,' she huffed out, slumping back into her seat whilst tightening her grip on his hand.

Fireworks lit up the sky over the sea, causing Rory to jump, as he was too busy staring at Tilly to notice that the display was about to start.

Bobby came over and handed out some hot chocolate drinks before sitting the other side of Rory. 'Ooh, I love fireworks.'

Rory watched Tilly's mouth as it met with her cup. He leaned closer to her, gaining her attention. 'Tilly love, I can't wait to get back to The Post Office Shop tonight.'

She snorted on her drink and coughed back the mouthful she had struggled to swallow.

He kissed below her ear, nuzzling into her hair, with a big grin on his face. Her hand reached up to stroke his cheek, and she turned so that their lips were almost touching.

'Why, what are you going to do, Rory Murphy?'

His mouth twisted to one side. 'Check out your kitchen chairs.' He pulled back to look at her. 'I'm pretty sure we can make our bonfire the biggest on the island.'

She slapped his arm and laughed. 'I swear to God, if you touch my…'

Rory grabbed her face and kissed her, silencing her immediately. An abundance of sparkles filled the dark sky, bringing it alive with noise and colour whilst two people beneath fell even deeper in love with each other.

'Rory, life is going to be so different for us both now. We'll have many nights like this.'

He stroked her hair away from her face, studying every inch of the beautiful woman he had been blessed with.

Never in a million years would I have ever believed I could be this lucky. Had someone told me a year ago that I would have someone look at me with so much love in their eyes, I would have laughed in their face. That type of thing doesn't happen to me. How is this happening to me now? How is it even possible to feel so completely in love with someone to the point where my heart actually hurts? I've never felt this way before. This woman owns my heart. Does she even know?

'Come here, Tilly love.' He gestured towards his lap.

Tilly happily obliged. Lifting the red check blanket from her lap, she clambered over to snuggle into his big chest.

Rory pulled the cover and tucked her back in, then moved his head so that he could lean in for another kiss.

The thin wooden poles holding the chair gave way, the legs cracked, snapped, and then the whole thing plummeted straight down to the sand, taking Rory and Tilly along for the bumpy ride.

'Ow!' Rory cried out as his backside landed in a thump.

Tilly's hot chocolate went up and then down, splaying out all over the blanket.

Bobby jumped out of his seat, gasped at first, then burst out laughing to the point he had to declare to all onlookers that he desperately needed the loo. And off he ran.

There was little in the way of dignity in the way that Tilly scrambled to her feet. She reached her hand down for Rory, and he clasped her small fingers, losing them in his palm, chuckling as he stood.

A few people close by clapped and cheered, and Tilly curtsied to them before hiding her crimson face in Rory's chest. He wrapped his arms around her and kissed her head.

They both glanced down at the broken deckchair and laughed once more.

'Well, I guess they won't be needing that one back,' said Rory.

Tilly giggled. 'A great addition to our bonfire.'

'See, now you're getting the hang of it.'

They turned to watch the rest of the fireworks display and didn't laugh again until Bobby came back, took one look at the broken chair, and cracked up once more.

20

Tilly

Tilly sat at a large round table in one of the barns on her farm. She was surrounded by her friends, Anna, Joey, Dolly, Tessie, and Josephine. All eyes were smiling down at Anna's baby girl, Harper, who was wrapped up in a lemon blanket, fast asleep in a big white pram.

Josephine stood. Her beady eyes peered down at the baby. 'She's blessed, this one. A happy life.' She nodded at Anna.

Anna smiled. 'Let's hope so.'

Josephine's wrinkly finger pointed her way. 'It is so. I know.' She looked over at her granddaughter. 'Joey, I'm going to have another burger.'

'Oh my goodness, Gran. I don't know where you put it.' Joey turned back to the table as her grandmother hobbled off towards Joseph at the BBQ outside. 'I swear, that woman could eat a whole buffet to herself.' She held her small baby bump and let out a hushed moan. 'I can't eat much at all lately.'

Dolly reached out and held Joey's hand. 'Aw, you'll get your appetite back soon enough.'

'I hope so. I've gone right off chocolate, and that doesn't help matters when I'm trying to bake in the tearoom. Josh keeps buying me sweet treats to try and tempt my taste buds, but it's not my mouth that has the problem. It's my stomach.'

'You just managed a vegan hotdog,' said Anna, wrinkling her nose.

Joey shrugged. 'Josh brought those. I like them.'

'Hmm, I had one,' said Tilly. 'It was okay. Reminded me of sage and onion stuffing.'

Tessie scoffed. 'Josh had me try a chickpea burger once. That was nice. Not going to lie, I wasn't expecting it to be nice, but there you go.'

Anna's husband, Jake, came over, checked on their daughter, and asked Anna if she needed anything.

'Ooh, Jake, you smell like bonfire.'

'That's because we were all standing around it a minute ago.' He looked over at Tilly. 'Rory's telling ghost stories, would you believe.'

Tilly laughed as Joey scoffed. 'Is that why you came in here, Jake?' she teased. 'Did you get scared?'

Jake grinned her way. 'I'm not scared. In fact, I think I might just go and tell him our very own Pepper Bay ghost story. The one about the woman in white who walks the cliffs every full moon.'

Everyone except Anna laughed. She tugged on his arm, lowering him to her. 'I haven't heard of that. Is it true?'

Jake smiled onto her cheek as he kissed her.

Tessie waggled one hand across the table. 'Ignore him. He's making it up.'

Jake straightened to go back outside. 'Yeah, but Rory doesn't know that.'

Tilly threw a napkin after him. 'Oi, you. Leave Rory alone.'

Anna turned back to the women. 'I believed him as well.'

Dolly gestured towards the opened barn doors and quietly laughed. 'Looks like Rory will too in a bit.'

The women muffled their laughter.

Oh, goodness, poor Rory. What will he think of my friends winding him up? Knowing him, he'll tell them a few stories of his own. No doubt come up with a severed hand in the school library or something. That'll bring Jake Reynolds running back in here.

Anna clasped one hand to her chest. 'Ooh, I don't like the idea of ghosts, especially one up on the cliff by Starlight Cottage.'

Joey breathed out a laugh as she flicked back her blonde hair. 'Don't worry, Anna, I can always send my gran up there to smudge the whole area. She'll send them on their way.'

'Forget about Rory, if you lot keep talking ghosts, I won't sleep tonight,' said Tilly, reaching for the bowl of ready salted crisps in the middle of the table.

Tessie gave her a dramatic wink. 'You could use that as an excuse to snuggle up to the big hunk of a man. Come on, Tills, strike while the iron's hot.'

Oh, if only you lot knew how much striking I do with the man. That'll keep you in gossip for the rest of the year, at least.

Joey screwed up her taupe eyes. 'I reckon she has already got him exactly where she wants him.'

Tilly cleared her throat whilst pointing at her chest. 'Erm, why has the subject changed from ghosts to my love life?'

Anna beamed widely. 'So, it is a love life then, Tilly?'

Dolly patted the table. 'Come on. Tell all.'

The women all leaned closer, and Tilly couldn't help but laugh at the curiosity burning deeply in their eyes.

'There's nothing to tell.'

Dolly sat back. 'Oh, like that, is it. That's fair enough. Early days, I'm guessing.' She glanced around the table. 'Well, I'm just glad there's another Irish person in the bay. It's nice to hear my own accent every now and again.'

Joey smiled warmly her way. 'You both have a lovely accent, and Rory's tone is so soft at times. I find him quite soothing.'

'He's gorgeous as well, isn't he?' said Tessie, glancing at the door. 'Nate reckons he looks a bit like Paul Newman.'

Joey waggled her glass of water as she went to take a sip. 'Hmm, I said that to Josh.'

Tilly nodded as she glanced over her shoulder at the doorway to see if he was there at all. 'A few people have said that. I'm not sure if I can see it myself.'

Dolly giggled, gaining her attention. 'That's because you're too close to his face, I bet.'

The women laughed, and Tilly waved them away.

Tessie bunched up her long red curls, tying her hair into a loose bun at the back of her head. 'Ask Josephine to read your palm, Tills. She'll let you know if Rory is *The One*.'

'Oh no,' said Joey. 'Don't let my gran get involved. She's already had his hand in my tea shop. Poor man didn't get a say.'

'No one gets a say with your gran,' said Anna, checking on Harper.

Dolly caught Tilly's attention again. 'You don't need a fortune teller, Tilly. If you want something, go for it. Don't wait around for someone to tell you what's coming your way. Make your own way. Take charge of your own life. That's what I say.'

Take charge of my own life. Yeah. I like that.

Tilly gazed around the barn as her friends chatted away merrily. She saw Rory walk past the doorway, and she couldn't help but smile to herself, only dropping her eyes when Tessie noticed that she was staring dreamily. Tessie gave her a cheeky wink, and Tilly couldn't help but laugh.

21

Rory

Sitting in a classroom, with twenty kids all staring directly at him was probably the most uncomfortable Rory had felt his entire life, and that was saying something, considering all he had been through. The fifteen-year-old boys were quiet, listening to Rory tell his backstory of crime and prison.

Josh was sitting on a chair at the back of the room with the school teacher, and Nik was leaning against a table beneath the large windows.

Rory had never held court before. He had worked with the younger men who came into prison, but that was mostly one-to-one. He started to wonder how teachers managed such an intimidating job. He glanced at the forty-something woman with the big round glasses and admired her for her bravery,

What was it that Dad used to say? Ah, yes, nobody intimidates you. You intimidate yourself. So, snap out of it, Murphy. Tell your story. One kid might just listen and learn something.

He cleared his throat and raised his head a touch, making eye contact with the lad in the second row, who looked the most laidback and unapproachable.

The boy held his stare and didn't move so much of an inch from his slouched position.

Well, there's one who thinks I'm a mug. Let's talk knife crime. See if that reaches him.

Rory lifted his top to reveal the scar on his stomach. He proceeded to tell the tale of a fight he had over a push and a spilled drink. Whenever he said it out loud, he felt stupid.

But he was eighteen back when the stabbing occurred, and he had no mind to talk things through with strangers in those days.

Nik joined in the chat, giving Rory some respite for a few minutes. He handed out leaflets about the dangers of carrying knives and told the teenagers that prison wasn't any fun.

Rory wasn't the only ex-crim in the room. Nik had done his time, changed himself, and went on to lead a life helping others. Just being in his presence helped Rory feel uplifted.

Thank God there are people like Nik in this world. Where would I be now if he hadn't stepped into my life? Could I ever be as good as him in this role? Look at the way they engage with him. He knows how to communicate with people, old and young.

He glanced over at Josh, and Josh offered an encouraging smile and waved him his way.

'You did well, Rory,' he whispered, as Nik was still up front, talking.

Rory took a deep breath as he lifted his hand to Josh and waggled it, showing his nerves. 'Tough crowd.'

Josh quietly laughed. 'At least they listened to your story. I think they just laughed at me.'

Rory playfully nudged his elbow. 'Might have had something to do with the part where you told them you're a rich kid.'

'Hey, we have problems too.'

They grinned at each other as Nik spoke about his time in prison, gaining more attention from the room.

Rory wondered what Tilly would make of the stories he had heard over the years. During his time locked away, he had pretty much seen and heard it all. Not much shocked him anymore. 'I'm glad Tilly's not here,' he whispered to Josh.

'If she was the judgmental type, she wouldn't like you at all.'

'Still, it's a lot to take in when it's all read out to you. Sometimes, I shake my head at myself when I hear myself speak about my past. I can't even believe half of it.'

'That's because you don't live there anymore, Rory. You can't relate to that life. That's why it seems so surreal.'

'Being here seems surreal. I don't mean here at this school. I mean the Isle of Wight.' He breathed out a laugh as he gestured towards the windows. 'I haven't even been in Parkhurst.'

Josh muffled his laugh as Nik's big dark eyes glanced their way. 'Well, we're heading to the Isle of Wight prison after lunch. You can see what it's like being on the other side of the bars.'

'Now, that should be an experience.'

Josh nodded towards Nik. 'Do you think you could take to this, Rory? We really could make a difference to someone's life.'

Rory slowly nodded. 'Aye. I want to help. I want to give something back.'

'Good. When we get back to Shine later, we'll brainstorm some more ideas with Nik. Figure out where we can fit.' He placed one hand on Rory's shoulder. 'We'll do some good, mate. We'll help with areas like addiction and education, and give people a chance at a new life. We both got a second chance, thanks to others. Now, we'll be the ones handing them out. We can only try.'

A wave of proudness washed over Rory, and that wasn't something that happened much to him.

I'm going to be like Nik, and the Sheridans, and Josh. I'm going to work hard at my job, be a volunteer at Shine, and let all that crap from my past go. The way is forward now.

171

And with Tilly by my side, I feel as though I can take on the world.

'What you thinking?' asked Josh.

Rory looked at the slouched boy, who had one hand dangling down, fiddling with the strap on his black bag. 'I'm wondering what that kid's hiding.'

'You can talk to him in a minute. Nik's wrapping up now.'

Rory approached the young lad as soon as Nik ended his chat and the teacher had thanked everyone.

The kids started asking Josh questions, mostly about being super-rich, and the boy who had caught Rory's attention tried to sneak out of the class.

'Hey, what's the hurry?'

The lad snatched back his arm from Rory's loose grip. 'I was going to the toilet.'

'I'll walk with you. I need the loo myself.'

The boy almost snarled as Rory followed him into the hallway.

'So,' said Rory, trying for casual. 'What's in the bag?'

The boy stopped walking and turned to face up to the man twice his size. 'What's it got to do with you?'

'Well, if you have a knife in there, I can help.'

The lad's right eye twitched, and his hand tightened around his school bag.

'It's okay, kid. We all mess up. You just heard my story. Well, some of it, at least. What Nik's trying to teach you is about making the right choices for yourself. Choices that make your life better, not worse. It's easy to choose the wrong path. Trust me, I know. But what I also learnt was that I can change my life at any given time. You can too. If you have something in your bag that's going to get you into trouble, we can sort that problem right now.'

Big green eyes peered up, filled with curiosity and a touch of fear. Rory knew that look well. The lad was an open book to the likes of him.

'So, what are you saying? If I had something illegal, you'd get rid of it for me?'

Rory shook his head. 'No. We'd go back to Nik and hand it over. He'll sort everything from then on.' He saw the boy lose trust immediately. 'Hey, kid, you won't find a better mate than that man. If anyone's going to have your back, it's him.'

The boy swirled his black trainer around on the matted floor for a second. 'It's not mine, you know. I found it.'

Whatever the lad's story was, Rory knew that the boy needed Nik's help. He only wished he knew the right steps to take, but he wasn't as well-trained as Nik when it came to procedure. He just hoped the boy wouldn't be immediately expelled, or worse, arrested.

'What's your name, kid?'

'Zane.'

Rory offered a warm smile as he gestured back towards the classroom. 'Come on, Zane, let's go see Nik. Tell him what you told me.'

Zane nodded and waited for Rory to take the first step. As soon as Rory turned his back, Zane shot off down the corridor at the speed of light.

Josh came out of the classroom and waved over at Rory. 'You all right out here on your own? What are you doing?'

Rory stared down the empty hallway and silently prayed that Zane would make better choices for himself at some point. He turned back to Josh and followed him into the classroom. 'We're never going to be able to help everyone, are we, Josh?'

'Nope. But how amazing is it that we can help someone, even if it's only one in a hundred.'

Rory smiled to himself. 'Yeah, that's true.'

I am that one in a hundred.

22

Tilly

Tilly was mooching around upstairs inside The Book Gallery, looking for a painting or print that reminded her of Rory. She wanted to put it up somewhere in her home so that she felt he was always around, which he was anyway, but she thought it would be a nice touch.

A box of small prints individually wrapped in cellophane caught her eye. She slowly flipped through, taking in the pictures of Pepper Bay.

'What you after, Tilly?' asked Scott, coming out of the shop's office.

'Oh, hiya, Scott. I didn't know you were in there. I saw Stan sitting downstairs at the till, so assumed he was here alone.'

Scott peered over the top of his glasses, gesturing towards the side room. 'I was just doing some online orders.'

Tilly glanced back at the box of prints. 'These are all lovely. Did you paint these?'

'I did some. Tourists kept asking Dolly if she sold any tea towels with the sights on them, so she asked me to make some pictures of local scenery. I got some prints made for a few other bits for her gift shop too.'

'Ooh, good idea. I'm looking for something that reminds me of Rory coming to the bay.'

Scott rubbed the back of his neck whilst chewing his bottom lip, deep in thought. 'Hmm, that's an interesting idea.' He stepped closer and rummaged around in the box. 'There are a few farm pics in here, but I'm now thinking,

175

what about one of a man on the ferry? That could represent. What do you think?'

Tilly's thoughts drifted to Rory coming over to the island with Nik. It seemed like forever ago, and she didn't know who he was when he took that trip.

Oh, Rory, what must you have been thinking. Little did you know, eh? Little did I know. Just one trip and your life can change so much. I did not see that man coming. I didn't see any man coming into my life ever again, but here we are. Here I am, looking for some sort of memorabilia. What's wrong with me? Am I really afraid that he will leave? I don't know. I just know that right now, I want a painting of his time here.

'Not a bad idea. Do you have anything like that, Scott?'

Scott shook his head as he squatted down to another box that was beneath a table. He pulled it out and flicked through some larger prints. 'I know I've got some of the harbour that Wes made, and there are definitely a few ferry postcard prints, that much I know off the top of my head, but I think they have more in the way of people and cars.'

'No, that's not for me. I want something that says, I went on a journey and found something new and now I'm happy.'

Scott breathed out a laugh as he stood. 'Well, that's specific.'

'I know, I'm being fussy.' She flapped one hand in front of her face. 'I just have a picture of Rory in my head, and it would be so nice to see that as a real-life painting. Oh, I wish I could draw. You're so lucky, Scott, to have that gift.'

'Thanks. I've never really viewed it as luck. It takes a lot of practice. Still, I'm always grateful that I can create pictures. It's so relaxing and really clears my head.'

'I listen to Kate Bush when I need to clear my head.'

Scott smiled as he nodded. 'Good choice. I don't mind a bit of "Babooshka" myself.'

Tilly laughed and tapped his arm. 'You know, if you have any pictures of her up here, I might buy them.'

'Not sure I have any pop stars.' He grinned and went over to a big book to flip through its pages that were filled with more prints of the bay. 'There's a lone man in a storm in here.'

'Oh, no. Not trouble. I want something soothing. Peaceful.'

Scott rolled his bright blue eyes her way. 'How about I paint one just how you see it. You can choose what size you'd like too.'

Tilly smiled warmly whilst clasping her hands tightly together in front of her chest. 'Oh, really, Scott. That would be lovely. But only if you have time. There's no rush.'

'I'll make it my next job.' He closed the big book, and Tilly could see he was studying her. 'So, how's it going up at Dreamcatcher with the new kid on the block?'

Just the thought of Rory brought air to her lungs. She knew there was a big soppy grin plastered all over her face, giving the game away, but she didn't care. She'd been friends with Scott Harper since they were children. He'd even married her little sister just to help make Luna's bucket list dreams come true. She had no shame in revealing her love for Rory in front of him.

Scott grinned. 'Well, I think that look in your eyes answers that question.' He dropped his smile for a moment. 'Seriously, Tilly, how are you getting on? I know it must be hard for you after Lucas.'

Tilly sighed deeply and leant against the doorframe. 'It's different, Scott, and unexpected, but I really like him. I think most people can see it in me, except my parents. I haven't told them yet. I think they see us as good friends and that's all.' She shrugged. 'Not sure, to be honest.'

'You trust him?'

'Yeah, I do. He's a good man, Scott. He's been through a lot during his life. Now, he's a changed man. Someone who has worked hard to be a better man, you know?'

Scott nodded and offered a polite smile. 'As long as he treats you right, Tilly, he's all right by me.'

'And how are things with you and Dolly?'

Scott's narrow smile widened as he nodded slightly. 'Now, that was unexpected. I'm glad I met her, Tills. She's everything and more.'

'I'm glad you're happy, Scott.'

'And I'm glad you're happy, Tilly. Just hurry up and tell your parents so that you don't have the worry of secrets hanging over you.'

Tilly giggled into her hand. 'I can't believe I'm fifty and still worried about telling my parents I'm seeing someone.'

'Yeah, well, parents have the habit of reducing you to a kid with one look.'

'Oh, isn't that the truth.'

I hope my parents are as okay about Rory as Bobby is. Surely, it won't be that bad. I know he has a past, but my parents are good people who give second chances. Maybe they have already guessed what's going on and are keeping quiet. Oh, I don't know.

Scott waved her towards the office. 'Come on. I'll stick the kettle on, and you can tell me your idea in more detail. I'll make some sketches for you to check out.'

'Ooh, lovely. And you can tell me some more about Lemon Drop Cottage. I hear you're having some work done on the roof.'

Scott laughed as she passed him by to enter the office. 'That's what I love about Pepper Bay, everyone knows your business.'

23

Rory

It had poured down pretty much every day during the second week in November, so Rory had no idea why Joseph had asked him to head over to the caravans with the hosepipe and wash them down. It wasn't that long ago he had given them a good scrub. Still, it was a dry day, plus, it was good exercise, so he connected the hose to an outdoor tap attached to a piece of wood coming out of the ground and got on with the task.

Humming a song his dad used to sing, Rory slapped a broom to the side of a caravan. He was finding the cleaning process quite therapeutic and smiled to himself at how content he felt working and living at Dreamcatcher Farm. Had someone told him ten years ago what he would be doing now, he would have laughed in their face. He had trouble believing it himself sometimes. He never would have believed any of it. Farm life was so far from everything he knew. Open spaces, a happy family, and someone loving him was even further away from what he knew as his life.

He took a moment to inhale the freshness around him. No longer smelling a farm, just a hint of sea salty air drifting by every so often. The taste on his lips was so familiar now, and a far cry from the flood of pollution he had grown accustomed to in London. There was nowhere else he would rather be. It blew his mind just how comfortable he was living in Pepper Bay. Living a whole different life to the one he had known before. He finally felt he fitted somewhere, and with someone.

'Hey, handsome.'

Smiling before he turned, Rory lowered the broom to the grass.

Tilly waggled a cloth shopping bag his way. 'I brought lunch. Thought we could share it in one of the vans.'

He propped the broom up beside the caravan, turned off the water, and then opened the door, letting her go first. 'You got time?'

'Yes. Mum's working in the shop for the next couple of hours.'

He helped her unload the bag onto the kitchen table. 'A whole two hours, eh?'

She giggled and wriggled further into his side as his arm came up to snake around her waist. They shared a quick kiss before their eyes went back to focusing on the table.

'So, what are you feeding me today, Tilly love?' He pulled out one item at a time. 'Pork pies, egg-and-cress rolls, ready salted crisps, strawberry magic potion…'

'That's for afters.'

'I'm thinking starters.'

Tilly laughed. 'You need to eat.'

'What I need is to kiss my girl.' Her soft lips upon his warmed his heart and overwhelmed him with love. He picked her up and carried her to the bedroom, getting stuck in the narrow doorway.

They both laughed into each other's necks, and Tilly scrambled down to her feet so they could make it over to the bed.

He watched her remove her wellies and flop to her side on the bed and beckon him closer.

Whoever brought this woman into my life, thank you. I don't know what I ever did to deserve such a wonderful person. Do you even know how beautiful your soul is, Tilly

Sheridan? Do you even know how much I love you right now?

'Take your boots off and get over here,' she ordered playfully.

'Aye, miss. I'm coming.'

He sat on the edge of the bed and pulled his jumper over his head, then kicked off his boots.

Tilly sat up and wrapped herself around his back, and he reached up and held her hand over by his shoulder. 'Have I told you how much I love you, Rory Murphy.' Her voice was low and steady and full of meaning that was strong enough to reach straight into his heart.

He moved his hand and touched hers with his cheek instead, closing his eyes for a moment to absorb her.

How is my life suddenly so perfect? I just can't believe it. Everything feels so surreal. I love her so much.

'Rory?' The sound was soft and warm by his ear. 'Can we talk?'

'Sure, Tilly love. What do you want to talk about?'

She pulled him down so that he was lying on his back. He smiled up into her dark eyes and tugged her dungaree strap, lowering her to his chest where she stroked over his tee-shirt with her fingertips.

'I want to talk about what's happening here with us. And I don't mean in this caravan.' She breathed out a laugh, and he joined her. 'I want to talk about how we feel about each other, how much of a future you want with me, and your farm job.'

He stared up at the white ceiling whilst focusing on her steady breathing pattern. He tightened one arm around her shoulder, holding her closer, and kissed the top of her head, getting a mouthful of hair for his trouble.

'I've fallen in love with you, Rory. I want you to stay with me forever, but I need to know what your plans are. Where you see yourself five years from now. Oh goodness, I sound like a job interviewer. Ignore that. I just mean…'

'I know what you mean.' He lowered his mouth to her hair again and silently inhaled. 'I don't plan on going anywhere, Tilly love. I want to stay right here with you.' He waited for her eyes to meet his as she rolled her head up his chest. 'I love you. You mean everything to me.'

She reached up and kissed his lips, and he actually felt like crying. Cupping her face in his hands, he pulled her back so they were face to face.

'If I can't work here full-time, then I'll find a job close by so that we'll never be far apart, okay. I'll do whatever it takes to keep you in my life, Tilly love. I promise you that.'

'You can stay working here, Rory. I'll speak to Dad. I know he'll say it's fine. You'll be one of the family. You're already family to me.'

'You're my family too, but I can't have expectations. I have to be realistic about this situation. Nik sets these jobs up as a temporary fix to help people like me get back on their feet. I can't expect your parents to keep me around just because we're a couple.'

Her smile widened so much, he couldn't help but grin back.

'We are a couple, aren't we, Rory?'

'Aye, miss, that we are.'

'We can talk to my family, let them know our situation, and see where we go from there.'

His brow creased as he thought about what exactly the Sheridans would have to say about his relationship with Tilly.

'I don't want you getting your hopes up. I might be good enough to give a temporary job to, but that doesn't mean I'll be good enough for you in their eyes, and I can't blame them either. I'm not the type of fella parents want with their daughter.'

She placed a finger over his lips, shushing him, and he kissed it immediately. 'You're a lovely man, Rory. And you're right, some people might judge you on your past, even I did with the laptop business, but you can't do that. You know more than anyone that you're not that man anymore. You have to stick up for yourself if anyone tries to tell you that you're still that messed-up person.'

'I just understand where they're coming from, that's all. I even understood when you did that to me.'

'I'm so sorry, Rory.'

'You let that go now, Tilly love. I know that was a one-off. But others will see the old me. That, I have to accept.'

'No. That's not good enough. Fight for who you are now. You have spent years rebuilding yourself. That deserves praise. You should be proud. I'm proud of you.'

He arched his brow and grinned. 'Yeah, well…'

Tilly kissed him and then lowered her head to rest upon his chest. 'I think my family will be okay with us, but if they're not, I don't care. Nothing will stop me being with you. You can move in with me and help me run the shop.'

Rory smiled into her hair and kissed her head. 'Let's just wait and see what happens when we break the news, but just for the record, I would give anything to wake up every morning with you by my side.'

There are not enough words to describe how that would feel. What a life with you would mean to me. It actually hurts to dream about it. Maybe this is why I've never bothered with dreaming about such things before. Christ, it makes me feel vulnerable. I have so much to lose all of a sudden.

They slowly stroked each other's fingers that were resting on his chest, and suddenly his hand felt damp.

'Hey.' He lifted her face to see the tears in her eyes.

'I feel a bit emotional,' she said with a laugh. 'I seem to cry a lot more the older I get. I never used to be a crier.'

He sat up, taking her with him, and held her in his arms. 'Everything's going to work out for us, Tilly love. You know why? Because we're both going to work really hard to make sure it does, that's why.' He felt her head nod on his shoulder.

'Please don't ever leave, Rory.'

Her muffled, broken voice hit him straight in the heart, and it was all he could do to stop himself from crying with her. He pulled her off him and looked her directly in the eyes. 'What we have established here today is that we love each other very much, are willing to do whatever it takes for us to stay together, and that I am never going to leave you.'

She sniffed as she nodded, meeting his chin with her forehead. 'Just the thought of losing you breaks me.'

He took a slow, deep breath. 'If my maker wants to take me, then there's little I can do about it, but I'm telling you now, that's the only way I'm leaving you.'

Her hand scrunched his top. 'Oh, we're a couple of old fools, aren't we? Is this what it comes to the older you get?'

'I don't know. They don't teach us about this in school.'

'You'd think we'd be better at all this love business by now.'

He huffed out a laugh. 'You speak for yourself. I've been banged up for fifteen years. I'm well out of practice.'

Tilly smiled and kissed his cheek. 'I know another area where you might want to practice.'

185

Rory laughed. 'Oh, is that right?'

Her face dropped as though realisation of her wording had just popped into her brain. 'Oh, no, I didn't mean you need practice. I meant…'

'No. You were right. I need all the practice I can get.' He peppered kisses along her neck and fought to hold back when she let out a soft moan of desire. He struggled to lower her straps, so she took over, then removed her top so that he could kiss along her collarbone. 'I. Think. I. Should. Practice. Every day.'

'Yes, definitely, every day.'

Her warm body closed in on his as her hands reached up to grip the back of his neck. The heat from her mouth upon his overpowered him, rendering him motionless for a second. She whispered his name against his lips, bringing his mind back to life. Within moments, he had stripped them both of their clothes and was leaning over her, kissing her with passion and need.

'Rory,' she murmured, twirling her fingertips in his greying chest hair. 'I need you closer.'

He glanced over at the bedroom doorway. 'Where's the magic potion?'

'Next to the pork pies.'

He burst out laughing. 'Aw, Tilly love, you always know how to turn me on.'

She smiled up at him. 'You couldn't bring me one in could you? I'm starving.'

24

Tilly

Not bothering to knock, Tilly barged her way into Rory's cottage to make them dinner. She figured he'd be in the shower by now, as it was his usual routine after work. She had it all planned. She'd join him under the trickling water, then cook dinner, then snuggle on the sofa, discuss how best to break the news to her family about their commitment to each other, and then head off to bed with him for the night.

What she didn't expect to find when she swung the door open was a strange man standing at the far end of the living room, pointing a gun at her.

It was as though time froze for a moment. Even her emotions had left the building. Rory's large frame instantly shielded her as the front door slammed shut, jolting her back to the land of the living. One of his hands was behind him, holding her wrist, and the other was stretched out towards the gunman.

'Put it down, Moss.'

Tilly had one eye peering around Rory's body. Her mind was whirling, trying to process the situation. Moss was looking back. She thought about how shifty Tuck had looked, and how this man looked as ordinary as any other in the street. There were no warning signs about him. Blonde hair, blue eyes, plain face, simply average, except for the fact he had a gun in his right hand.

'Who are you, love?' he asked. His London accent was soft and quite calm.

'She's no one,' said Rory. 'She's just leaving.'

Moss shook his head. 'We both know that's not happening. Now, Murphy, move.' He waved him to one side with the gun.

Rory remained perfectly still, and Tilly swallowed hard as she found her bearings.

'What's going on here?' She tugged Rory's arm. 'Rory? Who is this man?'

'I asked about you first,' said Moss.

Tilly took a step out from behind Rory, which he obviously wasn't happy about, judging by his face. She glanced his way before turning back to Moss.

'I heard him call you Moss, and I can see what's in your hand, but I want to know why you're here?'

Moss gave her a polite smile. 'I've just come to get my money from Rory, love. That's all. As soon as he hands it over, I'll be gone.'

'You mean, you'll shoot us then,' she said, drawing her experience on such matters from crime programmes she'd seen on the telly.

Moss shook his head slightly. 'No, I won't. Murder is not my style. I'm just here to get what's mine.'

'Then why have you brought a gun?'

A twitch of a grin hit the corner of his mouth. 'Because Murphy's not going to just hand it over.'

'Yes, I would. If I had it.'

Moss glared at him. 'Well, you haven't so far, but now *Little Miss* here has rocked up, you might reconsider.'

Tilly waited for Rory's eyes to meet hers. She wasn't about to move until he faced her.

'I don't have his money, Tilly.'

'Tilly,' said Moss.

She looked Moss in the eyes, trying hard to stay focused and not reveal the nerves darting around her heart. 'This is my family's farm, and we don't want any trouble here.'

He shrugged one shoulder whilst keeping his eyes on Rory. 'Suits me, love. I just came here for my money. Me and my wife need it, you see, to get out of the country. I wouldn't have come here otherwise, but I've got family too.'

Okay, he seems genuine. He doesn't even look angry, or miffed at all. Maybe he really will leave peacefully if we pay him. I have to try something. I can't let him hurt Rory.

'I have money,' she told him calmly. 'I have savings. You can have that if you promise not to hurt Rory.'

Moss smiled whilst Rory swiftly turned her way.

'You're not giving him anything, Tilly. Do you hear me?'

'It's alright, love. I don't want your money. I just want my own money that Rory has hidden away.'

Rory's face was filled with thunder as he spun back to Moss. 'How many times do I have to tell you, mate. I don't have the money. This is the first I'm hearing about there being any.' He looked at Tilly. 'As far as I knew, when we got caught, the police took the lot. Now, he's shown up telling me they only got half, and I've squirreled away the other half. But it's not true, Tilly. I don't have that money.'

Tilly was surprised to hear Rory's London accent slip in and out of his sentences. She had never heard him drop his Irish accent before. As if the situation couldn't feel any more surreal, he had to add that into the mix.

Rory looked quite adamant. 'I really don't have his money, Tilly.'

'So he says.' Moss sniffed and raised his gun hand slightly, causing Tilly's rapidly beating heart to accelerate to a speed she didn't know was possible.

Rory stepped in front of her, and Tilly felt her blood starting to boil. She moved away from the protection she had been given and raised her height as much as she could, standing firm, even though her legs were shaking and she was sure she might throw up at any moment.

'If Rory says he hasn't got the money, then he hasn't got the money, but if you and your wife still need some, take mine. I'm giving you a solution to your problem.'

'And that's very decent of you, love, but this is a matter of principle. Me and him go way back. You don't stab your mates in the back.' Moss looked at Rory. 'Murphy, we've known each other since we were teenagers. Why are you being this way?'

Rory scoffed. 'Are you for real, Mossy? You break into my home, threaten me with a gun, hold my girlfriend hostage, and demand money from me that I haven't got, and I'm being a way, am I?'

I wish he'd stop doing that London accent. I feel as though I don't know him anymore. Looking at that gun, I guess I don't. Is this really how his life used to be? Hanging out with people like Moss. Waving guns around as though that's completely normal. How is this my life? Is that gun even real? I hope not.

'This could have been over ages ago, Murphy, if you was just straight with me. I never brought her into the mix. She walked in. You know I can't let her go. If you cared about her at all, you'd stop pratting around and tell me where the stash is.'

'For the love of God, man. I don't have the money. And I'm telling you now, Moss, you're not getting a penny of hers.'

Moss started to show some agitation in his face. There wasn't much for Tilly to go on, but the man's calm face now held a slight scowl around the eyes.

He's losing patience, and we're running out of time.

She held on to Rory's hand. 'Let me just give him some money to go away. He doesn't believe you, but he's obviously desperate to leave the country with his wife.' She glanced over at Moss for confirmation.

He gave a slight nod, but Rory wasn't happy.

'Tilly love, this is between him and me, and if he points that gun at you one more time, he'll get more coming to him than money.'

Moss breathed out a laugh. 'Not lost any of your spark then, I see.'

Rory rolled his eyes his way. 'What do you expect from me? You're in my home, threatening my family. Know that if I get that weapon off you, I'm gonna kneecap ya.'

'Rory.' Tilly tightened her grip on his hand, but he kept his eyes locked with his old teammate.

Moss grinned at Tilly. 'Now you know why I need a weapon when dealing with him.'

'Nobody needs a weapon here,' she told them both. 'We can solve this. Rory, you have to let me end this my way. Moss, do you want my money or not?'

'How much?'

Good. Now we're getting somewhere. With a bit of luck, this will be over sooner than I thought.

Rory's lips pursed and his eyes squinted a touch. Tilly could feel the tension coming through his skin onto her clenched fingers.

'I have seventeen thousand pounds in my account.'

Moss scoffed as he looked at Rory. 'Seventeen grand. Is she having a laugh?'

What a cheek! Who turns their nose up at that kind of money? Wait, how much does he think Rory has hidden away?

'It's more than you came with,' said Tilly, struggling to free her hand from Rory's tightening grip.

Oh God, Rory. What are you thinking? What is your next move? I know you're planning something. Please be calm. Just stay calm.

Moss was mulling over the idea. No doubt weighing up his options and thinking about his wife.

Tilly felt a sudden wave of dizziness hit her. She moaned quietly and reached for her head.

Rory released her hand and gripped her elbows instead. 'Tilly, what's wrong?'

She closed her eyes, longing for a seat. 'I feel a bit dizzy.'

He pulled out a chair, sat her down, and went to the sink to get her a glass of water whilst Moss told him not to move. Rory ignored the demand, making sure Tilly got her water. He sat to her side, holding one of her hands. 'Small sips, Tilly love. When was the last time you ate something?'

'Lunchtime, but I don't think it's that, Rory. The doctor told me I might experience dizzy spells. There are lots of symptoms for the menopause. My mum used to get a bit lightheaded from time to time. I probably just need to get my iron levels checked or something, if it's not that. I'm okay.'

He gently brushed back her hair from her face. 'Okay, but food might help. A bit of bread and jam to tide you over.'

'What's going on?' demanded Moss, stepping closer, without passing the coffee table.

'Menopause, that's what,' replied Rory, opening the fridge for the raspberry jam.

'My wife's going though that too. You eat your bread and jam, Tilly. I don't mind. You see, I'm not a cruel man. We should all eat something. We're in for a long night.'

Rory stepped in front of Tilly as she lowered her head to her lap. 'What do you mean, long night?'

Moss shrugged. 'Well, she can hardly pop to the bank at this hour. We'll have to wait till they open first thing and go then to draw out the cash.' He shifted his head to get a better look at Tilly. 'Oi, what you doing with that phone?'

I've already sent a text to my brother, telling him to get the police, but you won't know that till they arrive.

'Internet banking,' she explained, looking around Rory. 'It's what you do nowadays. I can just transfer the money to your account right now.' She showed him the app on her phone. 'See. Give me your details.'

Moss frowned. 'What details?'

'Your bank details.' She shoved Rory out of her way to see Moss looking confused. 'Do you have an account?'

'I've just got out of a fifteen stretch, love. The only banking I know is that one that landed me inside in the first place.'

Tilly needed to stall for time. 'Okay. What about your wife? She must have a bank account. Or has she just got out too?'

Oh no, I didn't mean that to sound so awful. He's going to think I'm being a right nasty cow. He doesn't look too impressed with me. Apologise. Quickly.

'I'm sorry. That came out wrong.'

Rory took the phone from her hands and placed it face down on the table. 'You're dizzy. The banking can wait. I'll make your food.'

Moss pulled out his own phone, pressed on the screen, then placed it to his ear. 'Hello, babe. Yeah, I'm fine. He said he doesn't know about the missing money. Not sure. I usually know when he's lying, but then again, I haven't seen him in ten years. His missus is here too. She's offered me her savings to help us out. No. I said, no, didn't I? Listen to me, babe. I did not threaten her. She's just doing him a favour, ain't she. What? No. She's a bit dizzy at the moment. No, I didn't do anything to her. She's going through the change. Yeah, I know. What? No. Babe, seriously?' He held the phone out to Tilly. 'My wife wants a word.'

Rory stopped spreading jam and moved towards Moss before Tilly had a chance to get up. He passed her the phone.

'Hello, I'm Rory's girlfriend.' She felt pretty proud about saying that out loud.

The voice on the other end was soft and slightly broken. 'I'm sorry about my old man, love. He's not really a bad person, but he wants us to start fresh somewhere hot, and he was told Rory hid some of the money they stole all those years ago. He doesn't want it all, just his share. We're not greedy people.'

'Do you know he has a gun? Do you know he has threatened Rory?'

She sighed deeply. 'I know. I'm sorry, but we know Rory. He wouldn't just hand over that kind of money without a fight.'

What is she saying? Why do they think that Rory is so hard that he would need to be threatened with a gun? They think they know him, but they know a younger version, and Rory doesn't live at that address anymore. He moved out a long time ago, and they need to realise that.

'You knew the old Rory. He hasn't been that person for years. He's my Rory now, and this life of crime that you and your husband are still wrapped up in isn't the life for him anymore.'

The woman coughed for a while, then cleared her throat. 'My husband learnt his lesson too, love, but things have changed for us. We need to get away.'

Tilly straightened in the chair, avoiding eye contact with both of the men in the room. 'I understand that, but you have no right involving my man in your business. He walked away from that life years ago. He has a different life now, and I'll not let you drag him back into your world. Now, if you just give me your bank details, I can transfer over...'

'I'm dying.'

Tilly froze for a moment. Shocked by the blunt words that entered her ear. She glanced over at Moss, and by the look in his eyes, she could tell that he knew what his wife had just said. She rolled her eyes up at Rory, and he frowned slightly at her. The phone was still pressed against her ear. 'I'm sorry to hear that,' was all she could think to say.

'We just wanted somewhere hot to go until the end. Somewhere by a beach. Sea, sand, sunsets, warm air, you know.'

Tilly nodded.

I'm not going to cry. This isn't our problem. I can see where they're coming from, but they've gone about this the wrong way. But at least now I know neither of them have anything to lose. Knowing his wife is about to die, Moss might not think twice about shooting Rory, after all. Why would he? No doubt he cares little for his life now. Oh crap, the police will be here in a minute. What have I done? This isn't going to end well.

'I can help with that, if you take my money.'

'I don't want your money, love. We just wanted what was owed. What was ours.'

'Rory doesn't have that money. He thought the police took the lot.'

'Do you believe him?'

Tilly glanced down at the jam-smeared bread Rory placed before her. She grabbed his hand as he went to turn back to the sink. His eyes smiled her way. 'I do,' she said into the phone.

'Men lie to us, babe.'

'Rory has spent years reforming. He was a mentor for the younger men inside, and now he talks to kids through another organisation, helping them with their addictions and problems, and he's going to help older ex-offenders too. He is a good person trying to make up for all the bad things he did.'

'I'm glad he changed. Can you give me back to my husband now, please.'

Tilly handed back the phone, which Rory quickly took and gave to Moss. Rory then gave her a glass of orange juice and encouraged her to sip some whilst Moss was talking on the phone.

He sat by her side, holding one of her hands whilst staring into her eyes intently. When she met his stare, he mouthed the words, 'I love you,' to her, filling her heart.

She smiled and kissed his knuckles.

'Now, take a bite.' He held the slice of bread to her lips.

Tilly whispered over the top of the jam. 'His wife's dying. That's why they want the money. To get away. I don't think she has long left.'

The smile in his eyes disappeared as he glanced over at his old friend. He looked back at her. 'So, he's got nothing to lose.'

Tilly bit in her bottom lip as tears pricked her eyes. She squeezed his fingertips and tugged him a touch closer. 'I'm scared now, Rory.'

His hand brushed over the side of her hair. 'You're safe.'

She gave a slight shake of the head. 'You're not.'

'Don't worry about me, Tilly love.'

She watched the twinkle in his eyes return and was about to say something else when Moss interrupted.

'She won't take your money, Tilly.' He flopped to the arm of the sofa and banged the side of the gun against his head. 'What am I gonna do?' he mumbled to himself.

A thud on the front door made them all jump.

'Open up. It's the police.'

Tilly wasn't sure whose mouth had dropped to the floor first. Moss jumped up, held out his gun, and aimed straight at Rory. She threw herself onto his lap, but he quickly lifted her off and stood, shielding her once more.

'Who called them?' spat out Moss, edging backwards.

Rory showed his palms. 'Keep calm, Mossy. We can sort this.'

Moss had tears in his eyes. 'I'm not going back inside, Murphy. Not now. I can't. She needs me.'

You should have thought about that before you came here with your gun.

'We'll explain everything to them. I'll get Nik up here. He'll sort it. It'll be okay, mate.'

Moss waved the gun around. 'Oh, who are you trying to kid? We know what they're like, and I've got previous. They won't care about my situation. She's gonna die without me there holding her hand. Do you have any idea what that feels like?' He aimed the gun at Tilly. 'Do you want to find out what it feels like to lose the woman you love? Do ya?'

Tilly reached forward to hold on to Rory's hips. Willing him not to do anything stupid as the police continued to bang on the door. 'There's a back window.' She gestured behind Moss. 'You could run.'

197

It was the first time since she had met him that he looked disorientated, lost, and beyond angry.

'Or I could kill you. You called them, didn't ya? Pretending to call the bank or whatever, but you grassed me up and now my wife will die without me.' He held the gun up with shaky hands.

Rory pushed her back behind him. 'Stay calm, Mossy. It's me, Rory. It's just us, and we've got out of worse scrapes than this before. Now, there's the window. Use it. Get going. Go home. Go home, Mossy. Go see your missus.'

It wasn't working.

'I want to see your missus first.'

Rory's head shook for a second. 'That's not an option.'

'She's a grass.'

'She's my world.'

'Then you know how I feel.'

'Moss, climb out the window before they break down that door.'

He shook his head and sniffed back his emotions. 'I'm gonna kill her.'

Tilly couldn't see Rory's face. His voice was calm but firm. She was practically snuggled into his back, feeling every breath that he took.

'Moss, climb out the window. Last chance, mate.'

He scoffed. 'You reckon?'

'I'm coming over to you in five seconds flat, and you'll have to use every bullet you have to take me down before I get to you, and I will get to you if it means saving her. Your best option right now is to climb out that window and go see your wife.'

Tilly's breath had disappeared. Her fingers had turned white from gripping Rory's shirt so tightly. She placed her forehead on his back and closed her eyes.

Please don't let Rory die. Please don't let Rory die.

'Moss, if you were anyone else, mate, we wouldn't be having this conversation. Now, for the sake of what's left of our friendship. Disappear.' Rory's voice broke slightly. 'Please, Mossy. I don't want to fight ya. Not you. Don't make me do it.'

Tilly was desperate to see what was happening, but there was no way Rory was about to let her come out from behind him. Not in a million years. All she could do was silently will Moss to leave.

Go. Go. Please, just go. Leave us alone. Please don't hurt Rory. Just go. Do the right thing.

'Okay,' said Moss. 'I'll go.'

She could feel the tension in Rory's body settle a touch, which helped her to breathe out the breath that was lodged in her chest.

'Good,' said Rory. 'Now, hurry.'

Tilly wasn't quite sure what happened first. The door crashing open, Moss fleeing through the back window, the loud bangs, or Rory turning and diving over her blood-splattered body.

25

Rory

Nik's dark bald head was the first thing Rory's eyes focused on when he woke from the operation he'd had that removed the bullet from the top of his arm.

Where am I? Oh, yes, hospital. Right. I remember now.

'Oh, finally decided to wake up, have ya?'

Rory attempted a smile. 'What you doing here?'

'Well, I was eating your grapes.' Nik gestured towards the small fruit bowl by the side of the bed. It held three bananas, two apples, a plastic pot filled with blueberries, and a paper bag containing green seedless grapes.

Rory's head felt groggy, and his throat sore. He followed Nik's eyes. 'Just you is it?'

'Tilly's just popped to the canteen with her mum for a cuppa.'

Rory took a deep breath, feeling awkward and uncomfortable in bed. The hospital gown he was wearing was twisted around his waist, irritating him. He tried tugging at it to shift it to a looser position, but it didn't do him any favours.

Nik stepped forward. 'Try not to move too much, mate. Just rest for a bit.'

'What happened to Mossy? Richard Moss.'

Nik sighed deeply as he plonked himself down into a big blue chair at the bedside. It squeaked on impact, causing him to glance down at its front leg. 'Let's just say he won't be coming out for a very long time.'

Rory winced as he shuffled himself up to a sitting position. 'Ah, no. Such a waste. Do you know why he was at my place?'

Nik looked over and nodded. His dark eyes looked just as deflated as Rory's. 'I'm gonna have a word. See what strings I can pull about him spending time with his wife when it gets towards her time. Not sure how it'll go, if I'm honest. You can't shoot at the police and expect sympathy.'

I don't even remember him shooting at them. Just that gun going off and Tilly shaking under me. Bloody hell, Moss. So stupid.

'He was obsessed about money from our job. Do you know anything about that, Nik? I didn't know there was any money knocking about. I'd like to know where that went. Not that I want it, but still. It would be interesting to find out who stashed it.'

'As far as I'm aware, it's just a rumour. I've asked around, but no one's talking. I'm not done yet. I'm going to see what I can pull up from your old case. See what was said back then. What the Old Bill know. But I'm pretty sure there's no money, Rory. Moss was clutching at straws. Wishful thinking, I guess. Shame about his missus.'

Rory wished he had a cup of tea. His throat was so dry and his stomach felt a bit queasy. He glanced at his shoulder. 'I still can't believe he shot me. We used to be so close.'

'I don't think he was aiming for you. He told me he was shooting towards the door.'

Rory scoffed. 'Oh, lucky me.'

'Hey, Rory. At least you saved Tilly from harm.'

Christ almighty, I can't even think about it. If anything had happened to her, I don't know what I would do. I don't know what I would be capable of right now. What a mess. Is this the kind of life I can offer that woman? She deserves so much better than the likes of me.

He took a deep, calming breath, filling his lungs and relaxing the tension on his forehead. 'How is she?'

'Not bad, considering. Although, she might just still be in shock. It was a shock for all of us. I think she's more worried about you, Rory. Not too sure about the rest of the family though. I've been summoned to the farm by Joseph. I'm going over there later. I reckon they've had enough of criminals now.'

And they've certainly had their fair share with me around the place. I'm just like one great big magnet for crime.

Rory tried to reach for the jug of water by the side of his bed. Nik quickly got up and poured some out into a plastic beaker.

'Here, just sip some.'

'Cheers.' Rory wanted to down the lot, but did as he was told and took a small mouthful.

Nik sat back down, watching him as though he had a thousand things to say.

I don't know what you want to say to me, Nik, but I've definitely got something on my mind.

'I'm going to need your help placing me somewhere else, Nik.'

Nik got up to place the bag of grapes on Rory's lap. 'Here, have a nibble. Get some strength back. We can talk things through later.'

Rory popped one in his mouth. The freshness on his tongue was well and truly appreciated. He hoped it would help his stomach settle. Something had to. Maybe he would feel better after some food. He was kidding himself. Everything was a mess, and that was the real reason his stomach was playing up.

'I want to talk about it now, Nik. Get it over with. It's making me feel ill to the pit of my stomach.'

Nik sat back down, leaning forward. 'You really want out, Rory?'

'It's for the best.'

'Best for who? The way I hear it, you and Tilly Sheridan have been getting close.'

Close, huh? That's one way to describe it. What am I going to do without her in my life? She has to come first. Get a grip, Murphy. Come on. This isn't about you.

'I can't stay there any longer, Nik. Sort something for me, will you, please?'

'Got anywhere in mind?'

Rory pursed his lips and shook his weary head. Everything seemed a touch fuzzy, and his arm felt heavier than normal.

Nik patted his hand. 'I'll sort something for you, Rory, but are you sure this is what you want?'

I don't have a choice. This can't be Tilly's life, and I only attract badness and madness. I don't know how else to protect her. The thought of not seeing her ever again is breaking me in two, but it has to be done. I can't allow anything like this to ever happen anywhere near her again. She comes first. I'll just have to cope. Oh, Nik. Don't look at me like that.

'Do you really think the Sheridans are going to want me around anymore?'

Nik shrugged as he leaned back in his chair. 'I guess I'll find out later.'

'Well, let's be one step ahead. Get me out of there, Nik. Send me away, and make sure it's off the Isle of Wight.'

'Okay. I'll sort something as soon as I get back to the office, which is where I'm heading now.'

'What time is it?'

'Time you had something to eat.'

Rory took another deep breath as a wave of self-pity washed over him. 'Why can't I have a normal life, Nik? I knew it was all too good to be true.'

'Hey, you listen to me. None of this was your fault. You have got a normal life now. You can't allow the actions of others to make you think your life is bad.'

'My whole life has been down to the actions of others. I was conditioned to be bad by others. I attract badness, madness, and chaos wherever I go, and now look. Tilly could have been shot because I'm in her life. Shot! Of all things. You see how all my crap rubs off.' He shook his head at himself. 'When can I get out of this place?'

'I don't know. The doctor hasn't been round yet. You can ask when he comes to check on you.'

'I can just discharge myself.'

'No, you can't. You got shot, Rory. Rest for a bit, yeah?'

'If he had shot Tilly...'

'He didn't, so let that go.'

'I still can't believe I got shot. After that time I got stabbed years back, I did wonder if being shot hurts as much.'

'Well, now you know.'

Rory turned his head so that he was looking Nik directly in the eyes. 'Just get me out of here, please. And don't breathe a word of this to Tilly.'

'Are you actually gonna leave without telling her?'

Christ! I can't think about that. I just have to get out of here. This is killing me.

'Aye. I think that would be for the best.'

Nik scrunched up his nose. He didn't exactly look impressed with Rory's decision-making skills. 'Really? You don't think she deserves an explanation? If it were me, I'd want to know. You would too.'

'She'll cry, Nik. Beg me to stay. Do all those things that I would. I can't witness that. I love her. I'll not bring shite to her life ever again, and with me out of the picture, she's got a good chance of at least having a calm life. She doesn't need the trouble that comes with me.'

'Mate, stop being so hard on yourself. It wasn't your fault.'

First Tuck, then Moss. No. I can't give my past any more chances to pop up and hurt Tilly. If I'm not there, she'll be safe.

'Please, Nik. I've made up my mind. Either you help me or I'll go it alone.'

Nik went to say something but Tilly walked in. She froze in the doorway for a moment when she saw Rory was awake, then she propelled herself across the room to throw her arms around his neck.

Rory winced at her tight hold strangling him. 'Okay, Tilly love. Let me breathe, would you.'

Her tearful, smiling eyes was the first thing he noticed as she pulled away.

Nik stood. 'Right, I'm off. Got a lot on.' He nodded at Rory. 'I'll see you later.' He then turned to Tilly as she sat in his chair. 'I'll probably see you up at the farm.'

'Okay. Thanks, Nik, for staying.'

He said goodbye and left, and Tilly immediately grabbed Rory's hand, showering his knuckles with kisses.

I'm so sorry, Tilly love. I know I said I'd never leave you, but I have to. Please understand, I'm doing this for you. God, I love you so much. Don't cry, Murphy, for Christ's sake.

'Where's your mum? Nik said she was with you.'

'She popped outside to call Bobby. She'll be back soon. How are you feeling? Do you need anything? What can I do?'

He shushed her. 'Tilly love, it's okay. I'm fine.' He saw the tears leave her eyes to roll down her pale, weary face. 'Come here.'

She snuggled into his side and kissed the top of his chest. 'Rory, I thought…'

'Shh! I'm fine. We're both okay. It's in the past now, and Moss won't be coming back anytime soon.'

She moved her head to reach up and kiss his cheek. 'I love you so much, Rory.'

'I love you too. Come on, stop with the tears now.'

Because I can't take it. You're destroying me here. How am I going to walk away from you? Ah, hell, it hurts. It hurts so much.

She sniffed, grabbed a tissue from the box on the side, and wiped her eyes and nose.

He gently lifted her chin as though any other movement would break her. 'Let me look at you.'

'I'm all blotchy.'

'No. You're as beautiful as you always are.'

She gave him a light peck on his lips and stroked his cheek. It was all he could do to stop himself from breaking down as he closed his eyes and rested his face in her palm.

I'm going to leave you, Tilly love, and I can't bring myself to tell you. I have new plans now that don't include you, and you should know, but I can't do it. I can't bring those words to my mouth. You'll hate me, but that will be good. It will help you to get through this. I know you'll get through this. You have to. You have to get over me. You have to let me go. Christ, I love the bones of you, woman. Argh! This is killing me.

He opened his eyes and lowered her head back to his chest so that he didn't have to look into her eyes. There was so much affection in them beaming his way, and his heart could take no more.

May the Lord forgive me for what I am about to do to this woman. Please know it's in her best interest. I'm sure as hell not doing this for my benefit.

He lowered his mouth and kissed the top of her head and left himself in that position, not wanting to move. Not wanting to let her go. Not wanting to break her heart, or his own.

26

Tilly

Nik curled his fingers around the orange coffee mug on the table in front of him. The Sheridan family were gathered around the same table, all looking his way. Tilly knew that he knew what was coming, as she could see the deflated, redundant look in everyone's eyes just as much as him. They had already made up their minds about their relationship with Shine. It was just a matter of dotting the I's and crossing the T's.

'I'm sorry, Nik,' said Joseph, removing his arms from the kitchen table to settle back in his chair. 'We really have discussed this in length.'

Nik smiled sympathetically, and Tilly knew he didn't blame them. As a family, they had been through too much. She was the only one with a look of doubt, and yet she was the one affected the most.

Bobby brushed his hand through his hair. 'This feels really sad. We've been helping those in need for so many years now, and we carried on as a way to honour Lucas.'

'But no more,' said Lillian. 'This family can take no more, Nik. I know my old heart can't. If anything had happened to my daughter…'

Joseph rested his hand over hers on her lap. 'Tilly's right here, and she's fine. Let's not go down that road, love.'

Tilly lowered her head. For some reason she felt guilty and couldn't look her mother in the eyes. 'I'm so sorry, Mum.'

Joseph sharply turned her way. 'This isn't your fault, Tilly.'

'He's right, Tills,' said Bobby.

'It wasn't Rory's either,' said Jamie quickly, and all eyes were on him.

Nik swallowed hard. 'I don't know what to say about what has happened here over the last couple of months, but Jamie is right. None of this is Rory's fault.'

Tilly glanced around the table at the glum faces that told her they clearly had more to say but were keeping quiet on the subject.

Please don't let them hate Rory. I can't bear it. He can't help it if some crazy man breaks into his home and shoots him. Look at them. They're silently blaming him. What am I going to do? Will they let him stay here now? I'm not so sure. Where would he go? He has no one. I'm all he has now. I won't let them kick him to the kerb. I have to say something. This subject can't be left hanging.

'We need to talk about Rory.'

Nik sipped his coffee whilst looking straight at Joseph.

Joseph turned to his wife first, then his daughter before talking directly to Nik. 'We like Rory. He has worked hard, been respectful, and fitted in well with our community.'

'But?' Tilly knew one was coming.

Joseph swallowed. 'But, since he arrived, we've had a robbery and a shooting.'

Oh no, they're going to kick him out. He will leave. He won't go against their wishes. I know he won't. How can I fix this? I don't know what to say.

Jamie jolted from his chair. 'That's not his fault. He saved the shop from being robbed, and Tills from being hurt.'

Lillian reached out and touched his arm. 'Sit now, Jamie,' she said softly, giving him a gentle tug.

Jamie sat back down, looking at Tilly for backup.

She gave him a slight nod before turning to her dad. 'Rory saved me twice. He saved Kasey Renshaw. He's started working with Josh Reynolds on a project that helps older ex-offenders get back on track. He never invited Tuck or Moss to our home.'

Yes, Tilly. Good argument. Now what?

Nik looked over at Joseph. 'Rory turned his life around a long time ago. He isn't a bad person. I know sometimes we get duped over at Shine, but I'm telling you, he is one of the success stories we have.'

'I get that,' said Joseph, 'but that Moss fella wouldn't have come here if Rory wasn't here. I know Rory isn't to blame directly…'

'But you're going to blame him anyway,' scoffed Tilly.

Lillian shook her head. 'It's not like that, Tilly. We just want our family to be safe. It took a lot for all of us to start back with Shine after what happened to Lucas. What has happened here lately is all a bit too much. We have Jamie to think about too now. He's young and impressionable, and…'

'I'm all right, thanks.' Jamie folded his arms in a huff. 'And Rory taught me loads. He never told me to do anything bad, and he helped me ask Robyn to be my girlfriend, and he told me he loves Tilly. There's nothing wrong with him, and I want him to stay.'

'Dad?' Tilly waited for his response.

Bobby twiddled with his phone and Rex could be heard taking a deep breath.

'He loves you, Tilly?' asked Joseph.

She gulped as she nodded.

This wasn't how you were supposed to find out. We had a plan. We were going to tell you. Talk to you about our future together. Find a way forward. Now what, Dad? Does it even change your mind?

Joseph quietly huffed. 'We're not sure about this, Tilly. We've all seen you two getting closer, but falling in love? You love each other now? Your mother and I do like the man, we do, but we just don't feel comfortable with him around anymore.'

Something in her heart pinged. A stab of pain brought tears to her eyes.

Joseph had more to say. 'We've decided to end our relationship with Shine once and for all. Sorry, Nik. We're going to convert the three cottages into one house ready for when Rex moves here. He and Bobby can live there, or perhaps Jamie when he's older if Bobby wants to stay here.' He turned to Tilly. 'We're sorry, love, but our minds are made up. I'll not kick Rory out with nowhere to go. He can stay until Nik finds him a place to live.'

'He can live with me, Dad.'

Lillian shook her head. 'We would rather he didn't.'

'Tough, Mum. You don't get to tell me who I can live with.'

'This is still our land, Tilly.'

'Really, Mum? That's the line you're going to use on your fifty-year-old daughter. Your home, your rules. Just know that if I have to move out, I'll go.'

Joseph leaned towards her. 'There's no need for that. Your mother has had a nasty shock, Tilly. Have some understanding. We had a man here with a gun. Rory was shot. It could have easily been you.'

'But it wasn't, was it? Why? Because Rory covered my body with his own. He would never allow anything to hurt me. He loves me. He told me, and he shows me every day. You can kick him off the farm, but you'll never be able to remove him from my life. I'm never letting him go. And we were going to tell you all about how we feel. We really were. We have a plan to be together, and we were going to talk to you about us staying here on the farm together. But if Rory can't stay, neither can I.'

Nik took a keen interest in his coffee whilst Jamie smiled widely, Bobby wiped away a falling tear, and Lillian sighed deeply at her husband.

Rex's voice entered the kitchen. 'I think we should regroup in a week's time to talk this through. We're all still in shock-mode, and no one is thinking clearly right now. We believe Rory is a good man, but now is not the time to discuss his future on the farm. We need time to process. That's why I call one week.'

Joseph nodded. 'Good call, Rex.' He glanced at Lillian, and she agreed.

Bobby huffed out a sigh of relief, and Jamie got up and left by the back door.

'I won't change my mind next week,' said Tilly.

Her dad's eyes were gentle and kind. They twinkled her way, giving her some hope that he was on her side. 'No one's expecting you to, love. Rex is right. It's too soon to discuss Rory, but we have definitely made up our minds about Shine.' He turned to Nik.

Nik smiled softly. 'That's okay. On behalf of Shine, I would like to say thanks for everything you have done to help over the years. We're so grateful for families like yours. Places like this farm. You've been a real Godsend. Not gonna lie, we'll miss having the Sheridans on board. Just know, you helped a lot of people. You did Lucas and yourselves proud.'

The memory of being told that Lucas had been rushed to hospital with stab wounds flooded through Tilly. She stood, waved away her father asking after her, and walked out the back door.

The air was turning cold outside in the darkness. She sat on the step under a porch light and took a steady breath.

Oh, Lucas, what would you say about the state of things here? Your legacy has come to an end. Do you blame me for that? Is this all my fault? Why you, Lucas? Why did you have to get stabbed? All you ever did was help people. You didn't deserve to die that way.

She clutched at her chest and struggled to swallow air.

I love you, Lucas. I always will. I'm so sorry you're not here and I'm still living without you. I'm so sorry I fell in love again and have laughed again and felt happiness. It's not fair.

She looked up at the dark sky and focused on the biggest star she could see.

How about voicemail, Luna, you up for that chat? I don't know what to do right now. I don't know how to feel. I'm struggling to breathe. Lucas's death is running through my mind, and now Rory might have to leave. I can't lose him. He could have died trying to save me. I still can't believe he was shot. I can't believe how much my world has been turned upside down since he arrived. Oh, Lulu, he means so much to me. It hurts. It actually hurts when I think about him. If he's here. If he's not here. I'm a mess inside. I don't know if he's broken me or fixed me. I just feel so many emotions. I want his lips pressed on mine. His warm body over me. I need to touch his skin. Feel him. He's in my thoughts every second of the day. All I long for is to be in his arms. I can hardly concentrate while I work. I just about sleep, as all I want to do is stay awake and look at him whenever he's in my bed.

She lowered her head to her hands. 'How can one person have such an impact?'

27

Rory

As soon as Tilly had left the hospital, Nik walked in Rory's ward with a large black holdall containing everything that Rory owned. After secretly packing up the items, Nik went straight to Rory's bedside, as instructed, waited whilst the man got changed, and then drove him to the ferry port.

There was a long discussion along the way. Nik tried talking Rory out of leaving, but all of his attempts failed. No matter what angle he came from, Rory shut him down.

They said their goodbyes, and Nik handed over all of the information that Rory needed for his next destination. Rory was turning his back on the Isle of Wight, but not Shine. They were still helping him. Nik had placed him somewhere new where he could work and live and start over once more where no one knew who he was.

Rory stood on the ferry, staring down into the dark water beneath him.

Forgive me, Tilly. Please, just forgive me. Find it in your heart to know that I'm doing this for us. For you. God, I love you, woman. I can't breathe properly. Come on, get a grip.

He opened his mouth and raised his chest, drawing coldness from the early evening salty air into his tight lungs. The land behind him was shrinking as the ferry headed towards the mainland.

Blimey, the last time I was on this ferry I had Nik by my side, filling my head with optimism and farm life. I can remember laughing as we approached the island. What the hell was I doing going to the Isle of Wight? But there I was.

All aboard and looking forward to a new life. Little did I know back then. Little did I know who I would meet and what would happen. And now look.

What looked to be the start of something wonderful, something so incredible, was now just a memory. He'd already decided to lock that precious jewel away in the back of his mind as soon as his feet touched land. There was no way he could relive his time with Tilly. The mere thought of never seeing her again had ended him.

Rory had spent his time in Pepper Bay feeling sceptical. There was no way in a million years his life would pan out nicely. Good things didn't happen to him. Disappointment filled his soul. How could he have been so stupid? Letting his guard down like that. What was he thinking? He knew the setup. To not have expectations. But he went there anyway, actually believing he stood a chance at happiness. That his time had come. He had paid his dues.

The splashing of the water caused him to stir out of his trance with the horizon. He glanced briefly at the sky before looking back down at the motion of the inky liquid below. His jaw tensed as he pondered over the idea of what it might feel like to jump overboard.

Only Tilly would care. I suppose Nik too. Don't worry, Mum, I'm not going to do it. It's just a thought. Christ, it hurts, Mum. It really bloody hurts. I'm doing the right thing, aren't I? Oh, I wish you were here to guide me.

He sniffed back the cold air and pulled a tissue from his pocket to wipe his nose.

What am I to do, Mum? How am I going to manage without her? I'm being daft, I know. I'll be fine. She'll be fine. She's managed on her own for years, and I've been doing it all my life. At least she's got her family around her.

Back to just me then. I wish I never got a taste of her life. To know what a decent family is like. To know what love is like.

The laughter of a nearby couple made him glance their way. The taller man out of the two wrapped his coat around the other man and held him close. They smiled at each other and shared a quick kiss.

Rory looked back at the sea. His heart crumbled to a thousand pieces, and his mind went blank for a moment. A child's scream and a mother's yell woke him. He turned once more to the island whilst telling himself not to look back.

It's gone now, Rory. It's gone. Time to move on once again. Pastures new and all that. I have to think positive. What will the next chapter bring for me? How will this next job work out? I'll not get too close to anyone there, that much I know. It'll be for the best if I keep myself to myself from now on. Trouble won't find me if I hide away from the world.

His eyes went against him and looked back at the island. He quickly turned his body towards the mainland. If part of his mind was going to fight this, he would make sure the other part of his brain was under his control. His back was firmly blocking out his past, and his eyes had little choice but to look forward.

A jolt of pain hit him straight in the solar plexus, and a gut-churning knot squeezed his stomach. Watery eyes blurred his view, and a lump in his throat refused to be swallowed.

Oh, Mum, give me strength. Please, help me cope.

Rory felt sick to the pit of his soul. Nothing felt right. Almost misplaced, somehow. Never in his years had he ever experienced the feeling now crippling him. It was all he could do to stop himself from pulling out his phone and calling her.

Christ, Tilly. I love you so much. I'm sorry. I'm so sorry.
The rest of the ride seemed to be over within the blink of an eye, and Rory found himself moving without thinking. He shook hands with the man who Nik had meet him on the other side, got into his car, and was driven away.

The dark country lanes could have taken him anywhere. He didn't care. There was a numbness that had taken hold of his mind and body. There was no more thought process, just blind movement. Nik's work colleague was the Pied Piper, and Rory was the one being led away.

When the car finally met its destination, night-time had well and truly set in, so not much light revealed his new home. A dulled streetlamp stood alongside a red-bricked building that held four small apartments in a square shape. A long track led to a farm where he would be introduced to the owner first thing in the morning. For now, the man from Shine led Rory inside the bottom left flat and told him that Nik would call tomorrow.

Rory was once again on his own. He sat on a hard, thin-cushioned sofa and leant on its light-wood arm. He glanced at the radiator beneath the window and then to the bare magnolia wall across from him.

The place lacked warmth, comfort, and the homely touch of the Sheridans. But this was his new home now, and he'd better get used to it. There wasn't going to be snuggles and open fireplaces. No home-cooked meals and freshly laundered clothes. He wouldn't be up extra early to knead bread, and there was no reason for him to stay awake in bed either.

The rustling of bushes scratched against the window, gaining his attention. He sighed deeply and took his bag into the back room where a single bed waited to give him backache.

He sat on the edge, pulled his phone from his jacket, and double-checked it was switched off. Tilly wouldn't know he was missing until morning. How was he going to sleep tonight knowing what awaited her?

Ah, she's going to be mad. Stay mad, Tilly love. Hate my guts and move on.

He chastised himself for thinking of her. It wasn't allowed now. Not here. Not in the new place. The new life. He'd made the rules. Now he had to stick to them. Tilly Sheridan was in his past. All he had to do was forget about her. Remove her from his heart, or at least lock away the memory and hide the key. He was pretty sure she'd never leave his heart, so hiding her somewhere in there seemed the next best option.

Unpacking what little clothes he had, along with the laptop Josh had given him, was enough to make his heart weep.

There's not much to you, Rory Patrick Murphy. Never mind. How much stuff does one person need anyway?

He raised his pyjama top to inhale the scent he knew was embedded into the material. Her head had rested there the last few nights before he got shot.

Who the feck carries a gun in England? People I know, that's who. Oh Christ, my life will never change, will it? I'm not supposed to be happy. It's not my destiny. I'm going to be like that Littlest Hobo dog, forever wandering from town to town, with no real family of my own. Why am I suddenly caring about being alone? I've been alone my whole life. Dad loved me in his own funny way, but nobody else has bothered. She bothered. She walked into my life and made herself known. She took the time to see me. And what did I do? I ran away. I'm destroying myself trying to save her from my shite life. But what else can I do? This is the only way to keep her safe. She'll be all right. She has to be. Oh God, it hurts. It hurts so bad.

His body slumped down to the mattress, with the scrunched tee-shirt draped over his neck and chin. A tightness gripped his chest as air was trapped in his throat, and there was a heavy pain behind his bloodshot eyes. Tension filled his face and fists. He gasped quietly, filling his lungs, and fought hard to control his breathing. Lowering his face to his knees, he closed his eyes and buried his aching heart somewhere he hoped would never be found.

28

Tilly

All morning, the tears had fallen. From the moment Tilly found out Rory had left the hospital, she had called him, phoned Nik and Josh, searched Rory's cottage for clues, spoke to every member of her family to see if they held answers, and refused to open the shop. Her head was aching from overthinking, worry, and exhaustion.

Sitting on Rory's sofa, with her head in her hands, she cried again.

Where are you, Rory? Why have you done this?

She could feel her blood starting to boil. Swiping her phone from the coffee table, she called Nik again. 'I know you know where he is, Nik. Tell me. Please.'

'Tilly, you know it's against company policy. My hands are tied. I can't give out his details, and he doesn't want me to. Tilly, I'm happy to talk to you, really I am, but you can't keep calling me about this. I can't help you.'

She broke down again. 'Oh, Nik, please.'

He sounded just as upset. 'I'm so sorry, Tilly. I tried to talk him out of it, but his mind was made up. He believes it's for the best, for you both.'

She wiped her nose with the back of her hand. 'Oh, what does he know!'

'Tilly, he doesn't want you to be in danger ever again. He blames himself.'

'I know he does, the stupid fool, but this is his home. He belongs here with me now.'

221

'Look, Tilly, all I can do is ask him to return the next time I speak to him, but I don't want to give you any hope. He was adamant about his move.'

She nodded as she took a breath. 'Okay. Thank you.'

Silence filled Rory's cottage. No laughter from them both. No crackling fire. No wafts of dinner coming from the stove. Everything around her and inside her was empty, alone, and cold.

She checked her phone once more to see if any of her texts had gone through to his phone yet.

He's not going to turn it on, is he? Oh, Rory Murphy, you big idiot. What were you thinking? You need to come home. Please, come home.

An idea sprung to mind, so she jumped up quickly and headed for her house.

As soon as she entered the living room, she opened her laptop and booked travel tickets that took her all the way to the East End of London.

That's where he grew up. That's where he has gone. To the only other place he knows. He has to be there.

She didn't bother with accommodation, thinking little about staying overnight. Rory would be found, talked around, and fall back into her arms, and they would head straight back home. Simple.

I'm not telling anyone. They'll just talk me out of it. I'll text Bobby once I'm off the ferry. Let him know where I am.

She checked an online map of London.

How big is the East End? It can't be that hard to find him, surely. What was the name of that pub he mentioned once? Oh, blimming heck. Something about a ship, and there was an island. I remember that much.

She checked the map again and found a place called the Isle of Dogs. Poking her finger at the screen whilst nodding to herself, she thought that would be a good place to start. She looked up pubs in the area and found one called The Lost Ship.

Rory had told her about a time he was dressed as a pirate doing a fun-run for charity from that place. It had to be a local boozer for him. He had to live nearby.

Please, God, let him be around there. I just hope he hasn't gone back to Ireland.

She packed her handbag with all the essentials she thought she might need for her unexpected trip and headed straight for the tram.

It wasn't until she was on the ferry that she decided to let Bobby know. He wouldn't be able to stop her, but on the off chance that Rory returned whilst she was out there trying to find him, at least he would know where she was.

'Are you nuts!' Bobby was less than impressed. 'You've never been to London in your life. Do you even know where you're going?'

'I have a general idea.'

Bobby scoffed dramatically. 'I can't believe you've upped and left on your own.'

'I had to do something. I was going insane.'

'Where in London are you heading?'

'The East End. A place called the Isle of Dogs. I think he grew up near there.'

Bobby gasped, and she just knew he had slapped one hand over his mouth. 'Tills, I've heard stories about that part of London. You can't hang around there long. You don't want to be there come night-time. It's dangerous. The people who live there lock up their doors and windows by ten o'clock at night, you know. You can't walk around those streets then.'

She wasn't sure if he was trying to scare her into coming straight back or if that really was the truth. 'Don't be daft,

Bob. You watch too much telly.' She shrugged off the thought, but the scary seed had already been planted. It didn't matter anyway. Once she found Rory, she'd be safe anywhere.

Bobby stayed on the phone until she was on the mainland, then told her that he was worried about her losing battery life and being trapped in London forever without a friend in the world.

Tilly, on the other hand, wasn't as bothered. She had a friend who owned a property in London. If she got stuck at any time, she could call him and go to his place. Wherever Jake Reynolds' London apartment was. She had money and her bank card. There was no fear of trains or cabs. She was pretty sure she could get about without problems. She wasn't as stupid as her brother thought she was. There were plenty of hotels scattered around. Checking-in wasn't exactly rocket science. This thought process kept her calm on the long train ride to London.

I think I'll text Jake, just in case. Best to get his address up this way. He goes there for business some months, so he might even be around. Oh, no, wait. Anna's not long had their baby. I don't think they've moved from Starlight Cottage since. Never mind. I'll be fine. This will all be over soon. The big city can't be that hard to navigate, and Bobby's idea of the East End is straight out of Oliver Twist, so I'm not listening to him. I know that no one is going to be singing "Consider Yourself" to me. At the end of the day, people are just people, no matter where they live. I'll be fine, just as long as no one really does feel the need to pick a pocket or two. Oh, bloody hell, Bobby. Get out of my head.

She spent the rest of the train journey trying to telepathically contact Rory to let him know where to meet her. Anything was worth a shot.

There were some shops at the other end, so she grabbed some lunch, as she had skipped the meal due to excitement, worry, and exhaustion.

Sitting in the train station, eating a ham sandwich, drinking a coffee, and figuring out her next route, Tilly took a moment to calm her racing mind.

Blimming heck, I'm in London. Wasn't expecting that when I woke up this morning. Mind you, I wasn't expecting my man to have buggered off. I hope his shoulder is okay. Stupid git. I'm going to give him what for when I see him. I better see him. I could see a few things while I'm here. I've always fancied seeing Big Ben up close. I wonder how far away I am from it. Oh, Tilly, shut up. This isn't the time for a tour. I'll have to come back though. Maybe in the summer. Rory can bring me and show me around town. That'll be nice.

It was gone three by the time she found what she presumed was the right pub. It was an old place, with peeled paint and frosted windows, but when she went inside, mainly because her bladder couldn't hold on any longer, the inside felt warm and friendly. No one stopped talking to look her way, which she thought might happen. No one cared about her heading straight for the loo either. And the toilet was clean and smelled like fresh roses, which she thought was nice. She checked out the diffuser sitting by the sink to see it was from Marks and Spencer and made a mental note to buy one.

The bar staff hadn't heard of Rory Murphy, so she was out of luck there. A walk around outside, on the off chance he was out walking around there too, was the next idea she had.

A bench overlooking the River Thames looked inviting, and even though a chill was setting in, and she knew that it was about to get dark soon, she plonked herself down to stare over at a passing boat.

The calmness of the water soothed her just as much as if she were sitting on the beach back home. She loved watching water flow, whether it was the sea or a river. She sighed deeply and glanced up at the dull sky.

Oh, Rory love, where are you?

She looked at the many homes around her, from the tall apartment buildings to the smaller properties. Some of which looked too expensive for the likes of her.

'It's quite posh here. Rory said it was all graffiti and broken bottles where he grew up.'

I must be in the wrong place. Unless he was lying and is a secret millionaire.

She breathed out a waft of cold air as she laughed to herself.

Not sure where to head to next, but I better make a move before it gets dark and I end up having to fight my way back to Coney Island.

Her own joke failed to amuse her, as the thought of gangs suddenly appearing as the darkness crept in caused her heart to flutter, and not in any good way. Bobby's voice was in her head again.

She quickly headed for the nearest station, thinking that if she just got out of the East End part, she should be okay. She got on a train and headed west, knowing there were theatres that way, so her thought process went down the road that the area would have plenty of nice hotels nearby for tourists.

Perhaps it is for the best if I don't travel home till morning. I could check out Rory's pub again before heading home. I might have better luck tomorrow.

She wasn't very comfortable on the underground, but the train ride didn't take too long, and there were quite a few people around, so she felt she was safer than a Warrior hearing clinking bottles and wished that film would get out of her head. If she couldn't survive a day trip to London, she was pretty sure she'd never make it in New York.

The streets were still busy when she surfaced from the station, which helped calm her racing heart. No one was smiling at each other like they did back home, but she figured it was cold, getting dark, and people had places they needed to be.

Speaking of which. I need to find a bed for the night. I really should have done this before I left. I wonder if Jake got my message.

She checked her phone to see four missed calls from Bobby, and one text from Jake. She ignored her brother and waved at a passing taxi to take her to the address Jake had given her.

Oh my goodness, that taxi is turning around for me. I've always wanted to wave one down like they do in the films. I want to wave at one in New York too. Which other cities could I wander off to by myself? I could be one of those Eat, Pray, Love women. I wonder if he'll let me take a picture.

The driver of the London black taxi was happy for her to take as many photos as she wanted, as long as she paid the bill at the end of the journey. His meter was already ticking over, and Tilly was stunned by how much the short trip to Jake's posh apartment building cost. She tipped the young man what she thought was appropriate, hoping she didn't look stingy, and headed inside River Heights.

A middle-aged woman with large red glasses and frizzy grey hair smiled warmly at her. 'I'm guessing Tilly Sheridan.'

Tilly smiled back as she headed over to the large reception desk across the foyer. 'I am.'

'Mr Reynolds called a minute ago to let me know you were on your way. I have the key for you, but I need to see some ID first.'

'Oh, of course.' Tilly rummaged in her bag and pulled out her purse. 'I have my driver's licence. Is that any good?'

The concierge checked it over, nodded, and passed Tilly the key. She waggled a finger towards a lift. 'Top floor. It's the only one up there. The Penthouse.'

'Thank you.' She entered the lift and grimaced when the door closed and she saw her reflection in the mirror.

'Oh great. I look washed out.'

Oh no, I've got a bit of sandwich stuck in my teeth. Hope nobody noticed. That's going to show in my selfies.

A whoosh of air left her mouth in annoyance.

Her next gasp came when she entered Jake's large swanky apartment. 'Wow!'

Her millionaire friend had just moved up to the top of her Christmas card list.

Flipping heck, Jake! This is where you live when in London. Lucky sod.

She quickly went over to the window in the open plan kitchen to look down at the River Thames.

Nice view.

She stepped away and plopped her bag down on a shiny white table and jumped as the front door opened behind her. Not knowing whether to laugh or cry, she remained frozen to her spot whilst staring over at Rory in the doorway.

29

Rory

'What the bloody hell do you think you're doing, woman?'
Rory's tone was both astonished and annoyed, and he knew
it. He rubbed his hands down his sides, needing to remove
the irritation from his sweaty palms.

Tilly placed one hand over her mouth and dipped to her
left heel. Smiling through the cracks between her fingers, she
mumbled his name.

It was all he could do to stop himself from picking her up
and carrying her straight to the bedroom. The intensity sat
between them like a charge of electricity. Their eyes were
locked, and their breathing shaky.

*Oh Christ, Tilly, what the hell are you doing to me? I need
to get away. I can't look at her. She's breaking me.*

The silence was broken by her hand shooting out his way.
'What kind of adult runs away from home?' The snap and
losing half her smile jolted him.

'I... I...' He took a moment to compose himself. He
wasn't in the mood for a conversation. The bedroom was the
only thing on his mind. Seeing her naked. Feeling her skin
on his. The tenderness of her lips. The affection in her every
touch. She was staring at him. The pupils in her eyes had
widened so much, her chocolate eyes had been eclipsed. He
raced forward and grabbed her face in his hands and kissed
her hard.

Her mouth froze on his for a beat, and he wasn't entirely
sure if he'd made the right choice, but then she slid her hands
into his hair and pulled him closer, and he was gone.

'Rory.' The mumbling vibrated on his lips. 'We need to talk.'

Words weren't accumulating in his head. There was a thumping in his solar plexus and a heaviness further down. He couldn't talk. He could barely breathe. Lifting her, they stumbled backwards to the front door where he reached out to slam it shut. Her back was pressed up against the frame, and her mouth was trailing down his neck.

'Rory,' she mumbled again, this time sounding breathy and in need.

'Hmm?'

'We need to talk.'

Her lips were pressed back against his, giving him no room to reply. 'Uh-huh,' was all he could manage and all he wanted to say.

Their arms stretched up above their heads, fingers locked as tightly as their lips.

'Tilly love,' he whispered close to her ear, knowing the full effect of those words.

Her body was coming undone between him and the door, and when the warmth of her mouth hit his earlobe and his name was whispered, he was joining her. She was his and he was hers, and there wasn't a thing he could do about it, and right there, with her love embracing him, there wasn't anything he was going to do about it.

He teased her mouth with tiny nibbles on her lip which caused her to hold on tighter to him whilst breathing out his name over and over again.

I've fallen for you, Tilly Sheridan. I have really fallen for you. How did we ever get this far? How is this my life? How is she mine? Ah, Christ, I can't get a grip on this. I need her. God, I need her so much.

'Please tell me you have your magic potion in your bag.'
He felt her smile upon his cheek before seeing her face, and it warmed him. God, how that simple act of her smiling on his skin warmed him.

'I have a travel one. I bought a small container and squirted some inside.'

He couldn't help but breathe out a shaky laugh as they stumbled to the table. If there was one thing that woman could do, it was make him laugh when he didn't want to. She made everything normal. How could she do that with such ease? A look, a smile, her touch, some simple words. She got him, reeled him in, and owned him just with her presence alone. He was a prisoner again. This time, he wanted to be. She called all the shots. He could see his place in the hierarchy. He was weak. She was strong, but it didn't matter. He was safe with her. This was a person who would have his back, stroke his back, grip his back.

She rummaged through her bag with one hand, the other still clinging to him as though her life depended on it. Her fingertips grasping his lemon shirt, clawing through the material, causing ripples of adrenaline to shoot down his spine. She pulled out the plastic pot, grinned wickedly, and tugged him down to the floor, showing where she wanted to be. They both knew he had the strength over her to take charge, but he allowed her to manoeuvre him wherever she wanted.

'There are beds in here, you know.' His breathy voice barely laughed.

'I want you right here.' Her voice was filled with so much heat and authority, he caved instantly.

'Yes, miss.'

Her hands were on his jeans, frantically fumbling with the zip whilst he struggled once again with those damn dungaree straps.

'I'm going to start carrying scissors for those blasted things.'

She giggled and removed both their clothes with so much ease whilst still wrapped around him, he had little other option but to be in awe of her contortionist skills.

The warmth of her skin pressed against his caught his heart in his throat for a beat, rendering him immobile. The brush of her lips over his brought him back into the game. He rolled her over onto her back and pinned her arms above her head, kissing along her neck. Tasting her. Loving her. Absorbing every inch he could reach.

'No, Rory,' she mumbled.

He pulled away to look down at the beautiful face that he had missed so much since fleeing the Isle of Wight. 'What's wrong?'

She sat up, moving him with her. 'Nothing's wrong. I just want you to be on the bottom.'

He caught the relaxed smile in her eyes and leaned forward to kiss the corner of the sexy tug at the corner of her mouth.

'Help me on your lap,' she decided, wiggling her little travel pot, and he immediately obliged.

A few beats later and they were the closest they could be to one another, and Rory was lost in the moment. Sweat dripped from his brow into her hair as she clung on to him with passion and intensity. The feel of her fingertips gripping his back. Her tongue sweeping around his earlobe. Warmth from her heating body reaching his heart. She tasted of him. Salty skin mixed with oaky cologne. The softness of her hair was wrapped around his fingers at the base of her head, moving her face to his, finding her mouth once more, the sweetness of her tongue. He had no way to slow them down. He didn't want to. It was clear she didn't want to either. Her body was weakening as his adrenaline pumped. She cupped his face so their mouths would not part. Hot, shaky breaths taking everything they could from the other. He clutched her hips, pulling her closer, keeping her steady.

'I love you, Rory. I love you.' Her voice was weak but her words strong and filled with truth.

The rush of love that he held inside for her poured through him. 'Tilly love,' he managed.

Was the ceiling moving or was it the floor? Rory couldn't be sure what was making his head light and his eyes feel sedated. He flopped his arms around her waist and buried his face into her neck as she leant over his shoulder, her arms sliding down to his sides.

He swore under his breath whilst waiting for his heart to return to a normal pace. His lips were resting weakly on her neck, so he took advantage of his position and kissed her. Slow and steady, wanting more but unable to find the strength needed.

A gentle voice wafted close to his ear. 'I love you, Rory. So much.'

He held on to her as he flopped back to the floor, resting her spent body upon his chest, one hand moving her hair from her face, and the other stroking over her bare back. 'You're my world, Tilly love.'

'Then don't be a fecking eejit, and come home.'

All he could do was laugh until tiredness consumed him.

A moment of blissful silence filled the apartment, and Rory closed his eyes. It wasn't exactly comfortable on the hard floor, but he didn't want to disturb the hold they had on each other. Plus, he was too exhausted to move.

Her mouth brushed lightly across his chest, with her lips gently clasping and tugging at his wiry hairs.

Give me five minutes and I'll be back in the room. Maybe ten.

A slow smile crept across his face, tugging at his sleepy eyes.

I could actually spend every moment of my waking day just like this.

'What are you thinking, Rory?'

'That I want to do that all over again as soon as possible.' Her laugh vibrated on his chest, and he slid his fingers into her hair, only stopping thanks to a knot.

She raised herself to look down at him. The tease on her lips drawing him in. 'I think we'll try something else in a minute.'

'Is that right?'

'Aye.'

'I think we should go home, Tilly love. There, you can do whatever you like with me.'

'Not sure I want to wait.'

He arched an eyebrow in amusement. 'Not sure I want you to, but Josh is waiting downstairs in the car.'

Tilly frowned in surprise. 'Why is Josh waiting downstairs?'

'He was the one who brought me here.'

'From the East End?'

'No. From Cornwall.'

'Cornwall?'

'Aye, that's where I was.'

She flopped back to his chest, her hands reaching his shoulders, and her fingertips lightly brushing over his neatly-trimmed beard just along his jawline. 'Oh, flipping heck.'

He rolled his head so that he could pull her fingers into his mouth. She giggled and it filled him with need.

'Hang on a minute.' She pulled herself back up again to look at him. 'How did you get here so fast?'

Rory grinned widely. 'He's only got a fecking helicopter, hasn't he? Nothing has ever scared the bejesus out of me like that before. Well, except you.'

She tapped his cheek. 'Oi.'

He quickly kissed her hand, needing every part of their bodies to be touching. 'So, that's how we're getting home in a sec.'

'So, my home is your home then, Rory?'

'You, Tilly love, are my home.'

Tilly's eyes were suddenly filled with mischief. 'How long do you think Josh would mind waiting?'

Rory breathed out a laugh. 'How much travel potion you got left?'

30

There was something about Rory Murphy that had become addictive. Her very own brand of an Irish drug that she longed for every moment of the day. Tilly couldn't stop staring at him all the way home. Holding his hand. Stroking his arm. Needing him. Wanting his touch. Craving his existence. Her head rested on his body whenever it could. Breathing him in and not caring who was watching.

He didn't seem to mind. Often, his arm came up to wrap around her, drawing her closer, offering his wares. She was taking it. Taking it all. Everything that was available, afraid of it slipping away again. The mere thought brought her close to tears.

If a fight was needed, then bring it on. Tilly was ready to take on the world and its sister if need be. There was no way in a million years she was ever letting her man go anywhere ever again. The tear in her heart from his last trip still hadn't mended. It could take little else. Her life was hanging by a thread, or so it seemed. Life with him felt dangerous. Fluctuating between DEFCON levels.

His cool eyes gleamed her way over the course of their short journey home, sending silent messages. It's all right. It's all right.

Was it? She couldn't be sure. Was there a safety net beneath her tightrope? If so, she couldn't see it. He'd stolen it when he did a moonlight flit. Unbalanced, unsure, and unstable were words torturing her. Rolling around at the front of her mind, tapping at the back of her eyeballs, giving her a headache.

Do you need me too, Rory? Am I expendable? Don't you leave me again. I'll not have it, you hear me? Can you read my mind? Look into my eyes. Look deeper. I'm right here, you big idiot. You're loved. Loved by me, and I'm not going anywhere. We're a part of each other. We don't get to choose now. The deal has been done. I'm yours.

Arriving back at The Post Office Shop seemed like a dream. The living room was warm from the heating being left on, and the place held a hint of wild flowers. It was as though she hadn't left on a whim to travel blindly all the way to London to track down a love that had left her bleeding on the inside.

Cornwall, would you believe it! I swear, this man will give me a nervous breakdown. What do I normally do in situations like this? Fair enough, I haven't been in a situation like this before, but still. What eases me when rattled? I wonder how he would feel if I start blaring out Kate Bush? God, half my brain feels numb. I suppose I could lock myself in the loo and cry. That's another way to lighten the load.

Rory was waggling the kettle close to his ear over in the kitchen. It was the furthest they had been apart since Jake's apartment. But with the street door locked, she felt safe that he wouldn't run away. He wouldn't dare. She would rugby tackle him. Go straight for the ankles. That'll do it.

The doorframe gave her support as she quietly watched him move around her home with a sense of belonging.

'Cornwall, Rory?'

He turned and glanced her way for a moment before turning away again, hiding his face. 'Had to go somewhere, Tilly love.'

'No. You didn't.'

The warmth of his body comforted her like a hot water bottle as soon as she touched him. She snuggled further into his back, stroking his stomach and kissing the soft material of his top. His hands stopped making tea and cradled hers, lifting one to his mouth, tenderly kissing her fingertips.

Having an addiction was hard. Tilly was struggling to breathe normally. A new anxiety had taken hold. She was afraid of him. Afraid of what he had the ability to do to her. She had never been so vulnerable. It hurt. It really hurt. There was a damp patch on his shirt where her eye was smooshed.

So much for crying in the toilet. Oh, come on, get a grip. I'm getting a headache now. This is so unfair. Not sure if this is payback for something. Sure feels as though someone is out to get me. Too many people in my life have left me. First Luna, then Lucas, now Rory. Even two of my brothers left. I can't think about this. I can't let my feelings branch out. This is about him. And I cannot tread carefully. I can't live like that. So why the heck am I crumbling here?

'Please don't leave me, Rory.' She had no idea if he heard her. The words whispered out without her permission. She had barely heard herself. The thought was supposed to stay inside her mind, where it would be safe. She swallowed hard, attempting to disperse of the lump stuck somewhere between her throat and lungs.

Rory slowly turned. His hand traced over her jaw and gently tipped her face his way. 'Leave you? I want to marry you. Spend the rest of my life with you. Die by your side. Be your guardian angel. Meet you again in the next life. Tilly love, I'm never leaving you again. Wild horses couldn't drag me away.'

Her breath caught and her heart thumped as though an opponent had winded her in the third round. He took the tear that fell and carefully wiped it to one side. The tenderness in his kiss just beneath her eye completely melted her into a pool of sun-hit ice cream. Jelly legs were doing a good job of keeping her upright, but nothing was helping much with the constant flow of water from her tired eyes.

Rory scooped her up into his arms and carried her like a bride to her bed. She was placed on her side, then onto his solid chest, and there she breathed again. A proper breath. One that filled her lungs and flowed with ease, relaxing the restriction just a touch.

Tilly closed her eyes as his hand soothingly brushed her hair back onto the pillow behind her. Her fingertips scrunched his top slightly as the flutter of anxiety hit her insecurities. His words had been filled with so much meaning. A depth she hadn't witnessed in him before. Why was her heart struggling to believe him? She knew why. He'd already let her down, showing her it was doable. He could just up and leave anytime he wanted.

Wild horses couldn't drag me away. His words. He meant it. Feel it, Tilly. Believe him. Oh God, I'm so weak. I don't like this. This isn't me. Why has this happened to me? Why now? I'm too old for this shit. Whose big idea was it to bring another man into my life at this age? It's so cruel to give me love, then snatch it away. What did I ever do to deserve this? I've always been nice. Previous life? Was I mean back then?

She tightened her hold on him. Wanting him closer. Needing her fix.

A soft kiss met her head. Another gentle touch to soothe her aching soul. She needed calming. She needed a solid guarantee, but that was impossible. Sure things didn't exist. Life was unpredictable.

Grab him, Tilly. Take him while you can. Life is short. Love now. Love hard. Enjoy him. Don't be afraid.

It wasn't easy taking advice from herself. Her tear ducts certainly didn't get the memo. She needed to stop crying, but the silent tears continued to wet his shirt.

'I'm so sorry, Tilly.'

That didn't help. His voice was as lost and alone as she felt. All she wanted now was to join with his body once again and never part. Never. It was possible. She could live out the rest of her days attached to him.

I'm going crazy. This has to stop. What the hell's become of us? It took me so long to accept my life after Lucas died. I was in a good place for years. I want that again. I want to be sure of my life. To know where I stand. My feelings for Rory cannot control my life. I need my happy, settled life back. I need courage right now.

Their fingers curled around each other's, swirling around. Their sensitive stroking speaking volumes.

'I love you so much, Tilly.'

There it was again. His broken tone. Damaged goods. A crack in the bubble they had spent the last three months creating.

She lifted her head and shuffled her body up so that she could place her lips down upon his. There were tears weighing heavily in his eyes too.

'I've really hurt you, I know, Tilly love.'

There was no denying it. She gave the slightest of nods and then kissed him softly.

He nudged her nose with his own. 'It's killing me.'

This has to end. We need to move forward now. I have to be sane again. It's a miracle he came into my life. A second chance at love for me. I can't keep holding on to pain. He's here, with me, telling me he loves me. That has to be it. We're past the bump in the road. We have to see what happens next. There's always a next until the final show. He is my next.

One more step forward. That's all I have to think about. That one step.

'It's over now, Rory.'

'It doesn't feel that way.'

'I know. It will wear off, like when you wake from a bad dream.'

'I wish this was a bad dream.'

She kissed his closed eyes and waited until he opened them again. 'I can't begin to describe how much I love you, Rory. It's overwhelming me.'

His hand held her jaw. 'I feel the same way.' He then raised his brow as though a thought had occurred. 'It's going to be all right now. I promise.'

Yes, I think that too, but there's one other promise I need you to make.

'Will you promise you won't leave me?'

'Christ, Tilly. I've made some stupid mistakes in my life, so I have, but nothing comes close to the one I made walking away from you. I knew I'd made the wrong decision the moment I was on the ferry, but the stubborn part of me kept walking.'

'That's the part that scares me.'

They kissed slowly, softly. A steadiness took over. Tilly started to settle.

'Let me put a ring on your finger, Tilly love. It might help show you where my home is.'

'Marriage doesn't pin anyone down. Love does.'

'Love brought me back to you.'

'Love made me come looking.'

Rory smiled warmly. 'We're a soppy old pair.'

'I'm perimenopausal. I have an excuse for messy emotions.'

'Is that right? Well, I'm stupid-in-love with you, so that's my excuse.'

She kissed him, unable to hold back. His mouth was warm and tasted so familiar now. The kiss lingered, breaking records, breaking their lungs. Slow, strong, filled with intensity. It felt like years had passed by. They had to breathe. She had to speak. 'Is that our happily ever after, Rory, marriage?'

'No, Tilly love. We need to talk to your family. I need us all to be happy.'

That was a conversation she didn't want to have. Unsure of her family's thoughts. It could go either way. Her head dipped, weakness taking hold. Rory held her chin, giving her the strength she needed.

'Hey, whatever happens, it won't break us. We'll figure it out. I might not be able to make my way into their hearts overnight or even in a year's time, maybe never, but I'll die trying, Tilly love. I'll die trying for you.'

She snuggled her face into his chest. The bad dream was fading fast. His breathing was settling. She could feel the change. There was something appealing about his large hand covering hers. The swirling touch started again. Her fingertip lightly brushed back and forwards over his wedding finger.

That's where the band would sit, telling the world he has a home.

'Are you going to marry me, Tilly love?'

She pulled his finger to her mouth and rested her lips over the imaginary gold hoop. 'No, Rory. I don't want that to be what holds us together.'

'I understand. But just so you know, it won't be. It'll just be a bonus to be husband and wife. We've already got that, in my opinion. I'm going to give you that life every single day. So, no, we don't need rings or a certificate. It would just be nice to have that as well. But, if you don't mind, from this moment onwards, I'd like to start calling you my wife. In my heart, Tilly love, you are my wife. You are my world. You're everything.'

'Well, if that's how you really feel about it, I guess it wouldn't hurt to buy a couple of rings.'

The light touch of his mouth on her head made her smile, inside and out.

31

The moment of truth had arrived. A talk with Tilly's family was overdue. Rory and Tilly had left it to the next day, refusing to leave each other's naked bodies the day before. Plus, it was a chat they didn't want to have. Neither of them fancied their chances, so avoidance was a good-looking option.

'Come on, Tilly love, we cannot go on this way. It's time to face the music. Let's go see what your family have decided.'

Tilly huffed as she closed the door to the shop. The air outside was cold, and the darkness made it feel colder. 'It's almost December, Rory, and I still haven't put up a tree or any tinsel.'

He checked the door, making sure it was secure, knowing full well he would receive an eyeroll from her. 'Christmas, that's what you're thinking about right now?'

She shrugged as she took his arm and looked up to the navy sky. 'It'll be upon us before we can blink, you know. We have to be prepared. Plus, I want it to be special. It's our first one together.'

He smiled down at her, knowing she was just trying to distract herself from what was about to happen up at the farmhouse. 'We can sort a tree first thing tomorrow. What do you say?'

She snuggled further into his body. 'I say, I'm looking forward to it.'

'And I'm looking forward to our first Christmas together. You know, we'll have to start some traditions for ourselves.'

'Ooh, yes. What family traditions did you have? We can mix them up and add our own.'

Family traditions, now that's a laugh. Dad used to buy me a little something to open. I can hear him in my ear. That's from your mum, Rory. His new wife never bought me anything. Aunt Jean and Tim weren't too bad during the morning, but come lunch, well, I guess their tradition would be a drunken brawl, which ended up with them making love in the bedroom around ten minutes after they'd beaten the crap out of each other. I wonder if they're still together? How am I supposed to relay any of that to Tilly? My house was like the NSPCC Christmas advert, and I was the child in need.

'We didn't have any.'

Tilly tugged on his arm, bringing him to a halt along the pathway. 'You must have something.'

'Food, drink, sleep.'

'That's it? No board games, no sing songs, no particular time to open your pressies?'

The smallest of twitches hit the corner of his mouth.

Well, there was that time Jean hit the neighbour square in the face with a Monopoly board. All hell broke loose. The poor woman's nose was bleeding, her flea-bitten mutt was swallowing all the hotels, and Jean's boyfriend was pocketing the money as though it were real. I don't know why he thought that the game would resume at all. Fair play to Jean, she did apologise afterwards, and even shared her stout, which had she just done in the beginning, the fight wouldn't have taken place. But as my old dad used to say, you don't touch a drink that wasn't poured for you. That poor woman learnt a valuable lesson that day, that's for sure. Even I was never brave enough to swipe my aunt's booze.

'No, Tilly love. So, it'll be nice to have some festive traditions with you.'

Her face came alight with warmth and cheer. 'We can buy some new decorations. Ones that are just ours. The Sandly Christmas Market will have some nice bits.'

'Sounds like a plan.'

She took a deep breath that he noticed as they carried on walking up towards the main house. 'We have plans then, Rory?'

Ah, she's feeling insecure again. Why did I have to go and ruin it? Why did I ever think that leaving would solve anything? Well, there's only one thing for it, I'll have to tell her every day for the rest of my life how much I love her.

'I love you, Matilda Moon. All my plans are with you.'

The fact that she pulled his head down so that she could kiss his cheek, snuggle into his side, and hold one of his hands up to her neck filled him with joy.

They both stopped just short of the farmhouse and stared at the front door for a moment.

'I feel like a teenager, Rory.'

He breathed out a laugh through his nose. 'I know what you mean. You wouldn't think we're grown-ups, the way we're acting.'

Tilly held her head high and puffed out her chest. 'You're right. I'm fifty, for God's sake. I'm not about to be told by my parents who I can live with.'

'Hey, it's more than that. Come on. Let's go hear them out.'

She stopped him taking a step forward. 'Rory, I'm telling you now, if we have to leave, we're leaving. Staying on the island, just not here.'

246

I am not letting you fall out with your beautiful family over me. I'm going to do everything I can to fix things here. This is about you, not me.

'Tilly love, let's not jump ahead.'

'Okay, Rory. Let's do this.'

Because they were expecting them, the Sheridans were all there, sitting around the large kitchen table, with what looked like a giant picnic laid out.

'Can I eat now?' asked Jamie, eyeing up the potato salad.

Lillian patted his hand away from the food whilst Joseph gestured to the empty seats.

'Sit down, Tilly. You too, Rory lad.'

Tilly went to speak, but Rory gave her hand a gentle squeeze and led her over to the chairs.

'Now,' said Lillian. 'I'm not going to talk to you both as though you're a couple of kids, but at the end of the day, this is my home and my daughter.'

Rory tipped his head. 'I understand.'

'The thought of someone hurting my baby all because of you…'

'Rory saved her,' said Jamie quickly.

Lillian placed her hand on his arm. 'I know, Jamie. Let me finish.'

All eyes were on Rory, and he was feeling the pressure of being in the spotlight. He wasn't one for being a beacon, always preferring to go unnoticed. But this time he was the subject, and he knew all too well how that felt. The judge, the jury, the audience, they were all watching, listening to the facts, the evidence, the witnesses. Checking out exhibit A, B, and all the rest of the alphabet. The time on the old wagon-wheel clock ticked high up on the wall. Counting down. Waiting for the final verdict.

247

Joseph cleared his throat, shifting not only his phlegm but the atmosphere in the room. 'We believe you love Tilly, and we believe you're a changed man. We know it wasn't your fault your friend came here after you.'

Jamie huffed. 'But? There's a but coming.'

Bobby flapped his fingers at the boy, shushing him, clearly wanting to hear more.

'There are no buts,' said Lillian. 'We want to clear the air, not attack Rory.' She moved in her chair so that she was directly facing him. 'Son, you've done no wrong since the day you arrived. We were upset about our daughter, and there were a lot of what-ifs flying around. We've had time to calm down and think things through.'

'And?' asked Tilly, squeezing Rory's hand tightly beneath the table.

He wiggled his fingers in an attempt to free them from her tension. Her big dark eyes briefly flashed his way before turning back to her mum.

Blimey, it was a lot easier standing in front of a judge than Tilly's folks. That jug of water is starting to look refreshing. I think I'm about to have one of Tilly's hot flushes in a minute. Oh, Mum, where are you now? Are you somewhere in the room?

He glanced over Lillian's shoulder, figuring if his mum was with him, she'd be right there, no doubt glaring at the woman who was about to throw her son out with the rubbish.

Easy, Mum. It's not over yet. But my life might be if Tilly doesn't stop squeezing the blood out of my hand.

'Mum?' she questioned, clearly irritated.

'We're happy for Rory to stay on here.' Lillian glanced at her husband, and Joseph nodded his agreement.

Bobby quietly clapped his hands together in front of his chest as Jamie leaned over and hugged Rory.

Well, what can I say? I wasn't expecting that. Nothing usually goes right for me. I can't believe they're giving me a second chance. Maybe with them it's a third chance. I don't even know. I don't know what to say. At least Tilly has freed my hand.

'As much as I want to say thank you,' said Tilly, leaning on the table. 'We weren't going to let you rule our lives.'

'We know that,' said Joseph.

'But I didn't want Tilly to fall out with her family. You mean everything to her.' Rory smiled her way. 'And she means everything to me. I never expected to end up here, and I sure as hell never expected to fall in love. Tilly has given me a new life, and you all have given me time and patience and a helping hand. I'll always be grateful.'

Joseph gave a slight nod and a small smile.

Jamie beamed up happily at Rory. 'You can work with me tomorrow.'

Joseph raised a hand. 'Wait just a minute there, Jamie. We haven't spoken about full-time work yet.'

'That's okay,' said Rory. 'I wasn't expecting you to keep me on. I always knew it was just a helping hand you gave out here. I can look for work. Josh Reynolds has already said he'll get me in up at Pepper Pot Farm. I can...'

'Work here with us,' said Lillian, cutting him off. 'You're a Sheridan now. The Walkers can find their own staff.'

Joseph caught his eye. 'That's if you want to continue working here, Rory lad. It's up to him, Lillian.'

Lillian flapped one hand. 'Oh, I know, but it's what we do here. We work together.'

Jamie tugged his arm. 'Please stay working here, Rory.'

He could see Tilly out of the corner of his eye, smiling his way. Of course she would want that too. He didn't need to

249

hear her opinion on the matter. It was written all over her gorgeous face.

Well, Rory lad, what do you want to do? Is farm life for you? Is this where you get to live out the rest of your days? Are the Sheridans really your family now? Will you truly be happy here?

He glanced at Tilly, then at Joseph. 'I'd very much like to stay working here. Thank you, sir.'

Tilly looked at Rory as though he was the best thing since sliced bread, and it warmed him to know he had made her feel happy.

'So, Rory can work with me tomorrow,' said Jamie, looking every bit as pleased as Tilly.

Tilly turned his way. 'Half day for Rory tomorrow. We're going to buy Christmas decorations for the shop and our home.'

Lillian's eyes widened. 'So, you're moving out of the cottage then, Rory?'

'Yes,' said Tilly, before he could draw breath. 'You're going to convert them anyway, and we want to live together.'

I knew something would go wrong. Something always goes wrong for me.

Joseph nodded. 'That's right. We're going to make the cottages one house. You could move in there once it's finished, if you want. See how it goes. It'll be bigger than the flat above the shop. Otherwise, Bobby and Rex will probably live there one day.'

Bobby shook his head. 'Oh, but I love this place.'

Lillian laughed at her son. 'Or Bobby and Rex will just live here.'

Jamie laughed. 'I can live there with Robyn.'

'That's a nope,' said Bobby, frowning over the table at him.

Jamie raised his arms. 'Hey, there's no point it going to waste. And I didn't mean now. I meant when we're older.'

Tilly reached over and tapped his back. 'The time it'll take Dad to build the place, you'll be old enough, so don't worry.'

Rory sat back in his chair and listened to the friendly banter fly back and forth in the Sheridan kitchen. Their voices were never raised. Their problem-solving skills deserved an award. And the love they had for one another was heartwarming and a pleasure to witness. He smiled to himself and slowly rolled his eyes up to the ceiling.

Thank you.

The back door flew open and in walked Rex. The biggest smile spread across his pale face, and the widest of eyes twinkled around the room. 'Got room for a little one?'

Bobby gasped with surprise, slapping both hands across his mouth as Lillian and Joseph stood to greet the cheerful man.

'I was going to surprise you all on Christmas Eve, but I just landed a huge contract that will keep my business ticking over nicely for the next five years, so I thought I deserved a break. Plus, I'm Team Rory. I had to come and support him.' He dropped his bags and hurried his way into Bobby's waiting arms. They shared a quick kiss, then Rex beamed over at Tilly.

Tilly used her palms to gesture towards Rory. 'Ta-dah!'

Rex blew Rory a kiss. 'Ooh, so much better in the flesh.'

Rory smiled widely. 'Hello, Rex. Good to finally meet you in person.'

Rex flapped one hand whilst the other gripped Bobby's waist tightly. 'Darling, we have the rest of the year to get to know each other.' He turned back to Bobby. 'I'm staying till January.'

'And you're just in time for Christmas tree shopping tomorrow,' said Jamie.

Rex looked over at Rory. 'Ooh, are we all going?'

Rory smiled down at Tilly. 'Yeah, I guess we are.'

Rex reached over the table to grab a sausage roll. He stuffed it in his mouth whilst smiling. 'Wonderful. I do love a family outing.' He stopped chewing and glanced at Lillian. 'We are family, right?' He rolled his eyes back to Rory.

Lillian smiled. 'Yes, Rex. Rory's family now.'

Rex swallowed his food and shuffled closer to Bobby. 'Ooh, this is going to be the best Christmas ever. Now, why is all this food just sitting here? I'm starving.'

Rory watched him quickly sit down and plate-up some sandwiches. The rest of the Sheridans started their dinner, and he had little choice but to eat as well, as Tilly started to serve him.

She leaned over and kissed him tenderly on the cheek. 'Rory love,' she whispered, close to his ear. 'Save some room, won't you. There are strawberries for afters.'

* * *

If you enjoyed this story, why not come back for another visit to Pepper Bay with Ned, Elliot, Belle, and Rosie.

Pepper River Inn

There has been a longstanding family feud in Pepper Bay between the Renshaws and the Trents, and it's about to get even more messy.

Rosie and Belle Trent have just inherited their uncle's rundown hotel and have decided to see if they can rebuild the unloved business. They don't rate their chances of having a successful inn, not with the perfect one right next door owned by the brothers Elliot and Ned Renshaw.

The two sisters and two brothers aren't meant to be friends, so when Elliot saves Rosie from drowning and they fall in love, it's down to Belle and Ned to keep the family feud alive. All they have to do is continue to hate each other. How hard can it be?

Printed in Great Britain
by Amazon